FOOD
COMBINING
IN 30 DAYS

About the Author

Kathryn Marsden trained originally in hotel management which sparked her all-consuming interest in nutrition and food science. When her husband Ralph was diagnosed with cancer, she embarked upon an ambitious study of different dietary treatments to try to help him and became so enthralled by the fascinating potential of simple food substances in treating disease that she turned her attention full-time to the health, beauty and fitness field.

Kathryn went on to qualify as a nutritionist and continues to run a busy practice dealing with requests for help from people with a diverse number of illnesses and stress-related conditions. Her studies included physiology, anatomy, biology, biochemistry and the naturopathic and orthomolecular approaches to nutrition. She holds a Diploma in Clinical Nutrition and Nutritional Counselling. Also a freelance journalist, Kathryn has her own regular columns in professional, health and popular magazines and contributes regularly to a range of other publications. She is author of Thorsons' *The Food Combining Diet* and *Super Skin*.

She is a familiar voice on BBC, local and independent radio and television. She is a member of the Faculty of the The Tisserand Institute and teaches nutrition to students at the Royal Masonic Hospital and at Colleges of Further Education. Much in demand as an after dinner speaker, she gives lectures and seminars nationwide.

When she is not travelling, Kathryn returns to her home base in rural Wiltshire. She is a keen gardener and is ably assisted by her rescued cats, Sophie and Sylvester.

FOOD COMBINING IN 30 DAYS

KATHRYN MARSDEN

Thorsons
An Imprint of HarperCollinsPublishers

This book is dedicated to
Sonyia Woolnough
for her kindness and her expertise.
We are fortunate indeed to know you, Sonyia.

Thorsons
An Imprint of HarperCollins*Publishers*
77–85 Fulham Palace Road
Hammersmith, London W6 8JB
1160 Battery Street,
San Francisco, California 94111–1213

First published by Thorsons 1994
3 5 7 9 10 8 6 4 2

Recipes pp. 133–67 © Sarah Bounds,
except pp. 144–5, 147–8, 154–5, 162

Kathryn Marsden asserts the moral right to
be identified as the author of this work

A catalogue record for this book
is available from the British Library

ISBN 0 7225 2960 0

Typeset in Ehrhardt by Harper Phototypesetters Limited,
Northampton, England
Printed in Great Britain by
HarperCollinsManufacturing Glasgow

Contents

Acknowledgements

A manuscript can take not only years of research and writing but months of meticulous checking and editing. I consider myself particularly fortunate to have been blessed with an incredibly talented support team of advisers who help so willingly and selflessly with each new project. Their constructive criticisms and comments are of inestimable value and I am grateful to you all. Particular and very special thanks must go to:

Dr John Stirling
Gillian Hamer
Annie Runyard
and
Ralph Marsden — spellchecker and editor
extraordinaire!

Preface

No animal in nature ever eats such a haphazard comminglement of heterogeneity. It does not speak well for human intelligence that millions of men, women and children continue to eat such meals day after day and take drugs to palliate the resulting discomforts.

Dr Herbert M. Shelton,
Food Combining Made Easy, 1951

Food combining has been part of my personal and working life for many years and my faith in its principles as a way of eating for long-term health has never been daunted. Those who have followed some of my previous writings will know that food combining was one of the factors that helped in my husband Ralph's recovery from life-threatening illness. Since then, I've recommended its simple and effective actions to patients, physicians, students, colleagues and friends and have witnessed some remarkable mendings; improvements which, in many cases, defy all current *medical* reasoning.

Food combining's success as a safe and effortless way to lose unwanted weight is legendary — and particularly impressive given the fact that most dieters will probably have tried and failed with numerous dieting plans before they turned to food combining. Food combining has also helped people to overcome serious eating disorders which were triggered in the first place by over-enthusiastic yo-yo dieting and calorie restrictions.

Television 'exposés' and journalistic jibes which, from time to time, have a justifiable go at the dangers of yo-yo and crash dieting may, occasionally and mistakenly, stack food combining books in the same pile. But food combining is not about missing meals, cutting calories or giving up and suffering. It works for weight loss by increasing energy levels and upgrading the digestion. It is also in line with the official World Health Organization guidelines of recommending less fat, more fresh produce and more dietary fibre and has nothing whatever to do with disgusting diet drinks, slimmers' meals or low-calorie melancholy.

Food combining understands that, for many people who want to lose weight, it simply isn't enough just to eat less. Reducing food intake can be counterproductive if it results in unstable blood sugar, lethargy, exhaustion, uncontrollable cravings and bouts of bingeing.

Food combining allows you to lose weight whilst still enjoying healthy meals in healthy quantities. After a few weeks of food combining, cravings just don't happen because you never feel hungry.

It is impossible to explain the feeling that emanates from seeing someone who has suffered with serious weight problems or with a multiplicity of chronic symptoms, for months or more probably years, recover their health and well-being with nothing more than a change of diet and a sensible programme of nutrient supplements. But I can tell you that it gladdens the heart and lifts the spirit.

The modern — and perhaps rather fashionable — condition of 'food allergy' responds particularly well to the introduction of food combining. Many illnesses which were previously diagnosed as allergies are, in fact, disorders of a disgruntled digestive system. It is easy to label a food which 'doesn't agree' as a potential allergen but, in my own experience in practice, the vast majority of these have turned out to be nothing of the kind. Individuals who, BC (before combining) suffered from blistering digestive discomfort and other unpleasantries, have found that their 'allergies' cleared completely once their food was divided into digestible combinations. I am convinced that indigestion is a grouchy forerunner to many of our more serious ills.

Nevertheless, collecting all those food combining experiences, recording them into a computer, spending hours in the library, ploughing through mountains of medical journals and putting it all together in a book is a different matter entirely. Copious quantities of heart searching, *re*-searching, cursing, editing, sleepless nights, midnight oil and 5 a.m. alarm calls go into the production. Only time then tells how the finished product is received by those who really matter — the readers.

Within one week of the publication of my book *The Food Combining Diet* last year, we were flooded with letters and telephone calls of approval. In the process, my husband Ralph and I experienced a mixed bag of emotions; surprise, relief, pleasure, delight, satisfaction and joy among them. The most gratifying part of the project has been that we were able to give additional assistance to lots of people. Ralph has spent days of unpaid time on the telephone to hundreds of initially desperate patients and relatives who have been comforted by being able to talk to someone who really understands and makes time to listen. Where possible, I have been able to liaise with G.P.s, talk to consultants and to individual patients and pass on some of my experiences to them.

One particular call, typical of the many we received, came from a lady who had read, for the first time, about food combining in her daily newspaper. She rang to say that her paper was delivered at 8 o'clock in the morning. By 9.30 a.m. she was in the bookshop. Four days later she was food combining 'like a veteran'. 'Reading your book, it was just as if I was reading about myself. It's the first time anyone has ever understood my food cravings, my hypoglycaemia and my weight problem.'

Another lady told us: 'I've been ill for twenty years. My digestion has always been a problem and I've never been able to keep my weight down. The doctors think I'm crazy because they can't find anything wrong. Now I've been following your recommendations for four weeks and I feel like a different person. So well — and most definitely lighter.'

And this from someone who had received a less than enthusiastic welcome from her G.P. when she went to her surgery complaining of fatigue and overweight and asked if he thought food combining might be worth trying. She knew lots of people who had benefited from it, she told him. He had never heard of either Dr William Howard Hay or of food combining and therefore concluded that it would be a waste of time. 'Those who say it is successful must be mistaken since

it cannot possibly have any scientific basis in fact . . .
The only way to lose weight is to eat less.' Several days
later this witty (and I think courageous) lady presented
the doctor with a quotation which she had found in a
book at home:

> On 13th September 1765, people gathered in a
> field near Luce in France saw a large stone mass
> drop from the sky after a violent clap of thunder.
> The great physicist Antoine Laurent Lavoisier
> (regarded as the founder of modern chemistry),
> who knew better than any peasant that this was
> an impossibility, reported to the Academy of
> Science that the witnesses were either mistaken
> or lying. The Academy would not accept the
> reality of meteorites until 1803.

Point taken!

Many people have commented on the simplicity of
The Food Combining Diet, its uncomplicated set menus
and its four-week weight loss plan. Over 100,000 copies
were sold within the first few weeks of publication;
initial stocks were exhausted almost at once and at the
time of writing it has already been reprinted five times.

To fulfil the apparently endless requests for a
'sequel', *Food Combining In 30 Days* was born. This
equally easy-to-follow, one-day-at-a-time healthy
eating plan guides you gently to sensible and perma-
nent weight loss and restored vitality.

But *Food Combining In 30 Days* is much, much more
than just a guide to food combining basics. You'll find
sensible advice on exercise (and on the dangers of
overdoing it!), on stress management and many other
areas of health and fitness too. The 30-point

programme allows you to make up your own menus and introduces one key food combining rule or health tip every day. So even if you have never tried to food combine before, you'll be able to understand and benefit from its clear instructions.

You'll eat well and satisfyingly with no hunger pangs and no cravings. By the end of 30 days, you'll feel brighter, lighter, fitter and ready for anything. I know you'll enjoy it.

Kathryn Marsden
Wiltshire, England
July 1993

Nota Bene

Ask any of my colleagues, patients or students and they will tell you how much I loathe the word 'diet'. The term is confusing now that it is used so often to describe low-calorie weight-loss regimes. But finding a suitable alternative is difficult. Any use of the word 'diet' throughout this book which is made in conjunction with food combining refers specifically to the food needed every day for health and balance. In the same way that The Food Combining Diet _has no connection whatsoever with faddy eating or unhealthy weight loss,_ Food Combining In 30 Days _encourages moderation and variety and discourages excesses and extremes._ Food Combining In 30 Days _is a great way to get back into shape and to learn the food combining concepts at the same time. It is not remotely related in any way to crash dieting, to expensive or strange diet foods or unhealthy eating habits._

Learn to eat healthily for life, not just before holidays or after Christmas!

1

Food Combining

———————— ❧ ————————

How Are You Feeling?

— ❧ —

Notice in doctor's waiting room: *To avoid delay, please have all your symptoms ready.*

It is a sad fact of life that, when asked 'How are you?' most people will answer with politeness, rather than honesty, 'Fine thanks'. Few will really mean it. How many people do you know who can say they are honestly one hundred per cent healthy?

Despite advances in medical care, surgical techniques and general living conditions, full and complete good health is a rarity. Mild but persistent infections, aching joints, tiredness, indigestion and other irritating symptoms may not be life endangering but are curiously common; they are also, unfortunately, too often dismissed, ignored and left unattended and untreated. But 'putting up with' or 'living with' discomfort and dis-ease can create more stress, more discomfort and a veritable vicious circle of being permanently 'under par'.

What's Up, Doc?

Happily, the connections between low-grade health, mediocre immunity, stress, inadequate exercise and poor-quality diet are well established. Unhappily, however, when symptoms are presented to the doctor, the majority tendency is still to prescribe drugs as a first resort rather than a vitamin tonic and diet sheet. When symptoms are legion and indefinable, deciding what's really up can be a doctor's nightmare. Often, it's a case of being unable to find anything organically wrong or having no suitable treatment available but offering a palliative on a just-in-case basis.

Many people endure long lists of symptoms (like those described in the letters below) for years, the causes of which are never diagnosed and the reasons never explained. The patient may have no choice but to resign himself or herself to stoical suffering.

The German philosopher Immanuel Kant believed that 'Physicians think they do a lot for a patient when they give his disease a name' and it would certainly seem to be true that labelling an illness can help some people to cope better with a particular condition. But there is also the view advanced by the famous physician August Bier that it is 'more important to cure the patient than to make diagnoses'.

Diagnosis or no diagnosis, my experience with patients – and that of many of my colleagues – is extremely encouraging. Long lists of symptoms are frequently diminished or completely eradicated by the use of simple dietary changes and a few well-chosen, quality supplements. From the letters and telephone calls we receive, it is also clear that many people have restored their own health status just by following the health tips given in the books on food combining, the principles of which seem to have the capacity to heal a wide variety of irritating, long-established and ingrained conditions. It's interesting, too, to hear the constant clamour of people wishing that 'this kind of service was available in my doctor's surgery'.

Although I'm a nutritionist and have tremendous faith in food as a therapeutic tool, I do not hold the view that diet is a cure-all or that food combining fixes everything; rather that its use together with other lifestyle changes often has the power to *make well* – in many cases without the use of unnecessary medication. This is why *Food Combining In 30 Days* might be also described as 'Food Combining Plus', since it also contains a fund of useful health tips as well as plenty of easy food combining guidelines.

Even though food combining may not fit conveniently with current scientific or medical reasoning (after all, it has only been proving itself for about a hundred years!), there is no getting away from the fact that following its principles continues to help people overcome (or live more comfortably with) both minor and major illness.

Day One of your 30-day programme will give you the chance to put food combining to the test by noting down any symptoms which bother you in a specially designed questionnaire. This will enable you to monitor your own progress, for at the end of the 30 days you will fill it in again – and see just how much better you're feeling.

Food Combining Experiences

By the time I meet them, the majority of my patients have endured long-term discomfort, the after effects of major surgery or the side effects of a large number of drug medicines. Many have suffered with severe weight problems and followed an array of diverse but unsuccessful treatments where the only pounds they lost were from their pockets and purses. It is usually through disillusionment, desperation or following a referral from their G.P. or consultant that they decide to investigate the nutritional path.

The following are extracts from letters which I have received from people who have found my food combining recommendations helpful in resolving their own weight and health problems. Some were referred to me as patients, others made contact after listening to my radio phone-in programmes, seeing my magazine and newspaper articles or reading *The Food Combining Diet*. What the letters show is that no-one should underestimate the ability of food combining to resolve not only stubborn weight problems but also to relieve long-established infirmity.

Permission to reprint these letters has been given voluntarily and willingly by each individual concerned and I have undertaken not to divulge names or addresses without prior permission. The originals remain in my confidential files.

I take absolutely no credit whatsoever for the results that these people have achieved. My involvement was limited to giving them what I considered to be the best tools for the job — nutritious foods, healthily combined, and a few carefully chosen, high-quality supplements.

Their successful recoveries are due entirely to their own commitment and diligent effort in putting a few basic rules into practice. I am most grateful to these very determined and dedicated people for agreeing to share their experiences and I hope that, by including them, these personal testimonies may be of help to others.

Your dietary advice of last August, embracing the Hay diet, has absolutely transformed my life. My energy levels have improved 100 per cent, there are no more headaches or skin problems. The depression is gone and I just don't have to worry about gaining weight at all. Food combining has seen to that!

Several months ago I contracted a serious virus which affected my hearing and balance and my family and friends were becoming increasingly concerned at my deteriorating health. It is now ten weeks since I started your food combining programme and it is everything I could have hoped for. I am delighted with my progress – the head noises are diminishing, I am calm and relaxed and I have lost all my surplus and unwanted weight.

When I first met you in 1990 I had undergone surgery for testicular cancer; my left kidney and adrenal gland were also removed, as you know. All this was an enormous shock to my system, both physically and psychologically. I was constantly run down, suffered with frequent colds and other infections and had no energy. Over the last three years, your invaluable assistance has helped to boost my immunity against illness and assist in my recovery. What impressed me most about your advice is that it has been comprehensive and manageable rather than dogmatic or extreme. For anyone who has suffered illness, or even if they haven't, I wholeheartedly recommend your food combining books.

I am now 66 years old. Many years ago, I was diagnosed with Crohn's Disease which was pernicious and savage. I could no longer absorb my food and I lost several stones in weight. Prescribed steroids and other drugs failed to alleviate the symptoms. Over a two year period, I had several major operations which resulted in the complete removal of my large colon and part of my small intestine. In the summer of 1992, I began a new life on the 'Hay system' and a range of supplements. My recovery has been meteoric. I no longer take steroids, my normal medication is at its lowest level ever, I am back to my normal healthy weight and I have a new life ahead of me.

I am pleased to say that I am making good progress since I had a partial gastrectomy for stomach cancer. The dietary advice given to me by the hospital was pretty useless, but by adopting your food combining method, I have been able to learn to enjoy food again.

After suffering with anorexia nervosa for several years, I contracted a virus and was then diagnosed with chronic fatigue syndrome (M.E.). After a year, there was no improvement in the symptoms of lethargy and tiredness, digestive pain and muscle weakness. I could not get out of bed without assistance and was too ill to even sit up. At my first consultation you looked at my medical history, lifestyle and diet, recommended a number of nutritional supplements and put me on to food combining. Within a few weeks, my digestion had improved. After a few months, my body was back to its normal weight and all the other symptoms were receding. I am still food combining which has become a way of life for me. I am stronger and healthier and I look upon my new way of eating as an investment for a healthy future.

In 1987 I contracted a salmonella infection, which was treated with a range of different antibiotics. My immune system was very debilitated and I was very susceptible to repeated infections. I also suffered lethargy, digestive discomfort, bowel problems, heartburn and sleeplessness. You recommended that I try food combining and also suggested some herbs and other supplements. After only a few days on the new diet, the results were staggering, the most obvious improvement being the dramatically increased energy level. As time went on, indigestion and heartburn become non-existent and I was able to sleep consistently and restfully. I will continue to use your diet because it makes so much sense to do so.

Thank you so much for all the help and advice you have given me during the last two months. It is a joy to be able to go through the day without a headache after suffering them these last two years.

I felt I must write and thank you for all the help you have given Robin and me over the last few months. I suddenly realized the other day how much better he is looking and how much better I feel. I know the diet was started for Robin's benefit [Author's note: Robin has multiple sclerosis] but I know it has done a tremendous amount for me too and for this I am most sincerely grateful; my weight loss and sense of renewed well-being and energy can only have been instigated by you. The diet seems to have become a way of life and I now sincerely believe that you are what you eat.

Are You a Dieting Disaster?

❦

> The human waistline will succumb
> To such and such a diet,
> The ladies gnaw
> On carrots raw
> Their husbands will not try it.
>
> *Ogden Nash (1902–71),*
> *American writer of humorous verse*

Whether you are uncomfortably corpulent or just a little broad across the beam, it's likely that you have tried to lose weight before. And you are, understandably and probably, pretty fed up and disappointed about it. Well, hang in here. *Food Combining In 30 Days* is very likely to change all that. Learning to mix and match your foods correctly also means eating healthily and well. Bodyweight balances beautifully. Follow *Food Combining In 30 Days* and you'll be on the road to healthy eating for life. Just think of it: never having to diet again!

Untold Misery

Dieters dedicated to regimes of low-calorie misery are all too familiar with the 'eat less, feel hungry, lose control, overeat, binge, bloat, feel guilty' syndrome. Even if these poor calorie casualties manage to stay the course, it's a fact of weight-losing life that unrepentant pounds have a nasty habit of piling on again — usually helped by subversive night raids on the fridge or surreptitious indulgence in afternoon cream cakes. You may still be within your far-from-fulfilling calorie allowance for that day but the lack of nourishment at main meal times has left you hollow, hungry and desperate. Trouble is, the emergency supplies which your body craves are more likely to be sweet and empty calories, not nutritious and healthful ones. Yet again, your diet has been busted.

A Waste of Money?

Unfortunately, we seem reluctant to learn from our previous dieting blunders. Even though most of us know that the majority of miracle-promising weight-loss diets are doomed to failure long before they leave the calorie counter, there is an almost lemming-like addiction to trying the latest and allegedly greatest new one. Ironic, isn't it, that even though an average of £25 million is spent on slimming products in the UK each year, the failure rate for weight-loss diets is still around 95 per cent. A rip-off if ever there was one? No wonder dieting has been labelled a 'national epidemic'!

Dieting is Definitely Dangerous

Scientific research and population studies have proved, if proof were needed, that long-term food restriction results in lethargy, tiredness, depression and lack of energy. It also seems that dieters have poorer concentration and co-ordination than those with more normal eating habits. Apart from the emotional trauma of dreading meal times, the quest for the 'perfect body' can induce serious physical and psychological damage including faddy eating habits, cycles of starvation and bingeing, life-threatening eating disorders and an increased risk of grave diseases! Persistent dieting encourages large fluctuations of weight which can seem impressive when it's on the way down but can become psychologically demolishing when it's on the up.

Phenomenal Food Combining

Food combining has decades of success, thousands of dedicated followers and plenty of serious research to attest to its eminence. Although it is Dr Hay's name that is most often associated with its 'invention', it was in the 1850s and 1860s that doctors known as Natural Hygienists began to look more seriously at the natural dietary approaches which became the precursors to modern food combining (Dr Hay was not born until 1866 and was, in fact, a disciple of the very famous food combining expert, hygienist Dr J.H. Tilden). Simultaneously and subsequently, a number of other exceedingly eminent authorities and intrepid researchers — particularly Drs Herbert Shelton and T.C. Fry, Doris Grant, Jean Joice, Harvey and Marilyn Diamond, Leslie Kenton, Dr Keki Sidhwa and Norman Walker (who followed its principles and lived to the age of 109!) — have become prominent proponents of the art. Their detailed studies, observations and writings provide a legacy of healthy living laws which, as our letters on page 7 show, have helped many people to achieve their natural bodyweight and to overcome a wide range of illnesses.

Empty Promises?

It can be difficult to understand how a diet that doesn't cut calories can help anyone to lose any weight at all. If someone told you that you could achieve your natural bodyweight with a food intake that was not only tasty but filling, sustaining and about as far from low-calorie mayonnaise and low-fat fromage frais as chalk is from cheddar, you might not believe them. (I was going to say 'as chalk is from cottage cheese' and then remembered that, for many people, they taste the same.)

Healthy Scepticism?

I don't blame you for being sceptical about an eating plan that promises weight-loss on three full meals a day, allows between-meal snacks, encourages indulgence and doesn't ban butter, cream or sweet treats. But it *is* true – and especially so for those who have never succeeded at any other kind of dieting.

It's interesting that, despite all the evidence for food combining and against so many weird and less-than-wonderful diets, there are still one or two cookery and nutrition experts who dismiss the abundant benefits of separating proteins from starches. What I *do* object to are the sweeping statements made against food combining by those who *assume* it can't work but, in fact, have never tried it! Or who deny its benefits because it doesn't fit in with the model of their orthodox beliefs — or the particular diet they are trying to sell! As Harvey Diamond points out with such foresight in his excellent book *Fit For Life*, 'belief systems can be the biggest obstacle to one's progress. If the belief in something is strong enough, no amount of evidence or proof of its falsity *(or ineffectiveness)* can dissuade the believer.' He also reminds us that we have come to believe that medicine and medical technology can solve all our major health problems — which, of course, they cannot. Since so many of our ills are self-inflicted, it must also follow that the remedy is, more often than not, in our own hands.

Why Most Diets Fail

The inflexible medical and media maxim persists that to weigh less you must eat less. Fine and true — if your superfluous pounds are entirely due to eating more than your body actually needs and you have the willpower and stamina to stick to a less than inspiring list of decidedly dull diet foods. But for most dieters, this can be an uncomfortable case of *déjà-vu*. You know. You've been there, seen it and done it all before!

Most diets do actually work — providing you can put up with the boredom and the pain — but once they're over, back comes the unwanted baggage. What *is* the point?

Health at Risk

Apart from the havoc that this see-saw system can play with your lifestyle, it can also shorten your life! Studies show that yo-yo dieting increases the risk of serious degenerative disease including gallstones and heart attack; it upsets your hormones, your energy levels and your immune system too.

Negative Nourishment

Most weight-loss diets don't contain enough nourishment to sustain your stamina, your appetite or your blood glucose levels. Which is why, after only a few days, so many dieters are tired, hungry and plagued with hypoglycaemia (the debilitating low-blood-sugar disease; see pages 61, 83). Become a slave to dieting and it won't be long before your poor weary body will react by refusing to lose weight under any circumstances!

It's the Quality that Counts

In my view, good health and balanced bodyweight have more to do with increasing the *quality* of food than reducing the quantity. I also believe that if we attend to the quality of our food, the quantity will take care of itself. All too often, a food is dismissed by a desperate dieter because it is high in calories even when it might be loaded with super sustenance. Conversely, just because something is labelled 'low calorie' or 'low fat', it isn't necessarily healthy. One of my favourite examples is the case of the 'cream' cheese. Next time you are in a supermarket, check out the full-fat soft cheese and read the label. It should say 'Ingredients: Cheese'. Surprise, surprise. Then look at the half-fat (sometimes also called low- or reduced-fat) soft cheese and get wise to the ingredients: emulsifiers, stabilizers, flavours, colours, preservatives and a variety of ghastly sounding chemical names and numbers have been included to replace the missing fat.

This scenario applies all too often to other allegedly healthy items marketed supposedly in the interests of a calorie-controlled diet and a healthy heart – including plenty of so-called 'diet foods'. But the paranoic quest for fat-free fodder, like so many other dieting directives, has been taken to ridiculous and, in many cases, unhealthy extremes. One thing is for sure: heart disease and obesity are certainly not caused by a deficiency of E numbers! The healthier option is to enjoy real food – even if some is the full-fat version – but to eat less of it and leave the manufactured junk and artificial additives (especially artificial sweeteners) on the shelf!

Tubby and Toxic

There is a growing belief that the soaring consumption of artificial additives may be just one more contributing factor to obdurate obesity. Our modern lifestyle imposes upon us an increasing number of pollutants which we take into our systems each day. On top of these are the ones produced by the normal processes of metabolism as well as those that accrue from the build-up of toxicity in the cells. This kind of internal 'metabolic imbalance' is described graphically by Dr John Tilden in his book *Toxemia Explained* (published in 1926). Nowadays, it seems to be an increasingly common condition of dieters and those with digestive disorders.

Old cells die off naturally at the rate of billions each day and must be replaced using the vital nutrients from the foods we eat. If left to clog the system, waste products (which Dr Hay referred to as 'internal pollution' or 'autotoxicosis') sap your vitality and lead to lethargy and sluggishness. If more toxic wastes are accumulated than eliminated, some experts believe that the excess will translate as overweight.

A healthy body works hard and constantly to detoxify itself. Nutrients are extracted from foodstuffs which are then used to rebuild, repair and cleanse. In an unhealthy body consuming an unhealthy diet, getting rid of internal poisons is not so easy. There are just too many of the wrong foods and not enough of the right nutrients to keep the digestive system functioning efficiently. If the digestion is overloaded and over-stressed, then the body becomes exhausted. The detoxification plants and elimination routes are so congested and overworked that toxins remain in the body, snarling up the system and squandering stacks of energy.

Everyone Wants Energy

How many people do you know who *do not* use words like 'tired', 'run down', 'worn out', 'fatigued', 'drained', 'drowsy' or 'weary' when describing their usual state of 'non-health'. Not many, I bet? But it is possible to bring 'verve', 'vigour' and 'vitality' into the vocabulary simply by introducing some of Mother Nature's natural health rules into your daily routine. *Food Combining In 30 Days* shows you how following a fresh, clean, properly combined diet and regular detox programme can elevate energy and shift the stubborn ballast which has been inflicted by years of misguided dieting and energy-eroding eating habits.

Forget Calorie Counting

Food Combining In 30 Days chooses foods not by their calorie content but by their nutrient density. Calorie counting becomes a thing of the past, saving time, hassle and guilt! After all, if you are no longer concerned with counting the wretched things, you won't be reproaching yourself for exceeding some unattainable limit. And because correct combining leads to competent digestion, all that nourishment is put to proper use.

How Soon Will I See Results?

If you are familiar with reduced-calorie dieting, you will probably also be aware that weight lost quickly nearly always creeps back. Shedding portly pounds in too much of a hurry is, as I've explained above, not only dangerous but counter-productive too. No sooner have they gone than the beastly bulges are back.

Don't Be a Physical Jerk!

Everyone's body is different, with contrasting nutritional needs and a differing metabolism. Some people fight incessantly with the flab whilst others can eat for three and never put on an ounce. In other words, everyone loses or gains weight differently at different rates. To a certain extent, genetic disposition will determine your ultimate body shape so don't expect to be a size 10 in ten days, especially if you've been a size 16 or 18 for most or all of your adult life. And conversely, don't wish wistfully for weight-gain if you come from a family who are naturally narrow and lean. It's important to realize, too, that some people will never lose or gain, whatever diet they follow; you may have to face the fact that your hips are inherited and accept that unrealistic expectations make for miserable disappointment.

Whilst it isn't possible to alter your basic shape (unless you are into corsets, girdles and other breathtaking devices), you can — with the right kind of diet and exercise — strengthen muscle tone and improve the way in which your body deals with the calories it consumes.

Doing What Comes Naturally

Food Combining In 30 Days is a special programme which will support and sustain your system with proper nourishment and — gently — nudge your body back into shape. Don't be disappointed if weight-loss isn't immediate or staggeringly impressive. Most food combiners tell me that weight usually reduces at around one or two pounds per week. If you have been unwell, then any change may take longer. Mother Nature's innate common-sense seems to decree that healing has priority over slimming.

Overweight or Undernourished?

Being overweight doesn't necessarily equate with overeating; it can, in fact, indicate lack of nourishment if the body is toxic or is not receiving enough nutrients to enable it to burn off the excess fat. In other words, someone overweight may not be ready to lose weight (or an underweight one to gain) until 'repairs' have been completed. This has certainly been my experience with my own patients.

Brain Power

The side effects of healthy eating can even go to your head: people who nourish themselves properly are less inclined to anger and depression. They're more 'in control', have enhanced feelings of self-esteem *and* improved psychological functioning. So whether you need to lose pounds, stones or kilos — or just improve your health and energy — make food combining a way of life. Overweight or just under par? Go for food combining and in 30 days you'll be changing fatness for fitness. As our letters show, it can even help those who are underweight, too.

Underweight Skinnies — A Special Case

Whilst overweights may drool longingly at the Twiggy-like outline of someone half their size, being too thin is no joke. It can sometimes indicate a serious health problem: anorexia nervosa, for example, is a condition that requires specialist attention and treatment. Even here, however, food combining has proved itself to be truly beneficial (see Letters page 7).

A number of post-op patients seem to suffer particularly from an inability to gain weight, often aggravated by the calorie-obsessive advice dished out by the dietitian in charge of their case. I have had considerable experience of patients who have suffered substantial weight-loss following major surgery (for conditions such as Crohn's disease or cancer). I have also been privy to the diet sheets issued to these patients, which are designed specifically to encourage weight gain.

A typical list of recommendations will include quantities of high-fat, high-sugar foods such as cake, sweet biscuits, cola, lemonade, ice cream, fried foods, sausages, beefburgers, bacon, jam, chocolate, trifle, fruit pie, sponge pudding and pastries. Whilst I am sure that these experts mean such information to be used only in the short term, even the most dedicated junk food addict can see that few people just out of hospital are likely to respond favourably to this kind of counsel. To make matters worse, fresh fruit, vegetables, salads and water are often advanced as 'unnecessary' in these circumstances because they are 'low in calories'! There are even official Health Authority leaflets that support and encourage such nonplussing nuggets.

Many people made sick, queasy and debilitated by such advice have found their salvation in food combining. By enhancing the nutrient quality of the diet and improving the digestion, absorption of nourishment is increased. The ailing body happily puts the nutrients to work to repair the damage and enhance the healing process. Only after this has been done will there be enough sustenance to spare for putting back the weight.

In my husband's case, food combining coaxed him back to his normal weight in two and a half years! His argument against the hospital advice that he was 'far too thin' and should put weight on 'in a few weeks' was countered by the fact that he was alive and well. 'Skinny but breathing', as he put it! He feels that slavish adherence to high-fat, high-sugar foods would have limited his chances of survival. Ten years after his operations for stomach cancer and peritonitis, he remains fit, well and very happy and his weight is normal.

Perhaps we would do well to keep in mind one of the many prudent pronouncements of Martin H. Fischer (1879–1962) in his book *Fischerisms*: 'First need in the reform of hospital management? That's easy! The death of all dietitians and the resurrection of a French chef.'

Most important of all, remember that food combining is well known for its ability to balance bodyweight naturally without reducing food intake to ridiculous extremes. So, from now on, forget calorie counting and lock away your scales. You certainly won't be needing unstable and unreliable weighing machines!

2

The 30 Day Plan

———————— ❧ ————————

What is Food Combining?

∾

As far as I am concerned, no road that would
lead us to health is either arduous or expensive.
Michel de Montaigne (1533–92)

Food combining is a particularly enjoyable approach to
healthy eating for a healthier life and which has the added
benefit of being able to help you lose weight safely, simply
and sensibly — WITHOUT CUTTING CALORIES!
It is not a quick fix fiasco but a delicious diet for whole
body health which balances weight and promotes well-
being. And for those who don't need to lose weight, food
combining is still of inestimable value, increasing energy
levels, improving digestion and, for countless thousands,
relieving and resolving long-term illness.

The basic principles of this tried and tested way of
mixing certain foods in specific combinations are
usually attributed to Dr William Howard Hay, an
American physician who was born in Pennsylvania in
1866. Other nutrition experts have advanced and
augmented his progressive teachings, making food
combining even more suitable than ever for the hectic
lifestyle and health problems of the present day. The

result is one of the healthiest, most reliable, best known diets of all time.

Food combining acknowledges that certain combinations of food are digested with greater ease (and less stress on the system) than other combinations. Based on the formula of not eating proteins at the same meal as starchy or sugary foods, food combining improves digestion, enhances the absorption of vital nutrients and increases vitality. In addition and as a natural consequence of food combining, you will automatically be following the official guidelines on healthy eating; that is, enjoying more fresh salads, vegetables and fruits whilst, at the same time, cutting down on sugars, fats and refined and processed foods.

Food combining also helps the body to use its essential food supplies for energy and repair — not as a garbage truck for spare tyres!

Food Combining In 30 Days follows these very basic but extremely important maxims:

Starches and sugary foods should not be mixed with proteins.

Fruit should be eaten separately from proteins and starches.

Food Combining In 30 Days also helps you on the road to healthy eating by:

Increasing your intake of fruits, salads and vegetables.

Reducing your intake of processed and refined foods.

Showing you how to use food — and food combining — to enhance your health and well-being.

Food combining is not a temporary measure, a short-term programme or something that one 'goes on' and then 'comes off'. It is a set of sound dietary principles which, once learned, can be incorporated easily into your everyday routine. There is no pressure on you to achieve unattainable goals, nor are there any drugs, powders, slimmers' drinks or foul-tasting meal replacements to face. Food combining will help you to achieve and maintain a comfortable and healthy body weight and, at the same time, introduce you to a fund of valuable and helpful health tips and guidelines. A fabulous feast of delicious meals ensures that you will not feel hungry or deprived.

Diet is a fundamental contributor to health and fitness but is not the only factor. Stress management, relaxation and exercise are also vitally important aspects of healthy living. For this reason, *Food Combining In 30 Days* is more than just a simple guide to food combining and weight control. It's also full of facts about how to overcome cravings, relieve anxiety and improve digestion and contains a wealth of hints for your sustained welfare and well-being.

If you would rather collect compliments than kilos and prefer to feel fantastic instead of fatigued, follow *Food Combining In 30 Days* and swap the bags under your eyes for bags of energy. Discover that good health is achievable, that food can still be fun and that eating *is* enjoyable!

How to Use The 30 Day Plan

❧

There's nothing like eating hay when you're faint.

Lewis Carroll (1832–98),
Alice Through The Looking-Glass

Food Combining In 30 Days is the easygoing guide to food combining. No difficult dishes to produce, no cranky menus — just straightforward simplicity.

But it's not just about learning how to avoid foods that fight: it's the hassle-free way to healthy eating, renewed well-being and balanced weight control.

Every day gives you a new health tip or food combining guideline. Take things gently and ease yourself towards good health a step at a time. Don't try to take too much information on board at once. Understand each day thoroughly before moving on to the next instruction.

You'll have only one key point to remember every day and each step will build gradually into a natural programme for whole body health.

Don't worry. You won't be expected to food combine fully right at the beginning. But within a few days you should feel confident enough to use the Easy Reference

Chart on page 131 and the food lists on pages 125 to 131. Meal choices are left to you entirely. Divided into starch, protein and alkaline menus, you will find a wealth of healthy and sustaining breakfasts, lunches, dinners and snacks to choose from.

Do keep in mind that the food lists and recipes are suggestions of how to eat healthily and to avoid mixing foods that fight. If there is a particular food item that is not to your personal taste, then please feel free to substitute something else. All you need to remember is to swap protein for protein or starch for starch and not to combine the two at the same meal time.

There is no restriction on quantity and no need to weigh portions or count calories. Eat until your appetite is comfortably satisfied, not until you are bloated or unable to move!

Choose fresh fruits and vegetables whenever possible and use canned ones only when you have no other choice. Frozen vegetables make good reserve stores if you haven't had time to get to the shops.

At certain stages throughout the 30 days, you'll find a review of what you have achieved so far. If you've faltered on any particular day – or for some reason haven't been able to cover every point, then go back and repeat that day or week again. It doesn't matter at all if you prefer to extend the 30 days to 60 or even 90. *Food Combining In 30 Days* is not a competition or a race against the clock, just an enjoyable way to discover the nutritious benefits of really healthy food. The health tips and food combining guidelines should be fun and enjoyable – they're not part of a rigid regime with inflexible rules – and if you put them together they'll steer you towards super health and renewed vitality.

Week 1 (Days 1–7)

Learning to Eat More Healthily
(Preparing for Food Combining)

———————— ❧ ————————

A good Kitchen is a good Apothecaries shop.
William Bullein (d.1576)

Aims for the Week

This week you will discover that food combining is all about healthy and delicious meals. The first three days are important preparation days. On Day Four you'll begin to learn the basic food combining principles, but need not worry about understanding them fully just yet. You'll also be encouraged to cut down on packets, tins and take-aways and increase the amount of fresh produce in the diet. At the end of the week you'll find guidelines on how to begin to take a little exercise.

Day One – Taking Positive Action

Renewed energy and vitality begin right here. From today, your new way of eating will help you to feel fitter, stronger and healthier. Answer these questions to check out how you're feeling right now.

How do you feel in your clothes?
Comfortable? _____
Uncomfortable? _____
Restricted? _____
Wish they were looser? _____

Personal Symptom Analysis

So that you can record your progress, complete the following Personal Symptom Analysis, ticking any conditions that apply to you; if you don't want to write in the book itself, photocopy pages 33–34 and use those instead. Keep them safely; you'll need to refer to them again at the end of the 30 day programme.

Do you suffer with:

Regular headaches _____
Migraine _____
Indigestion _____
Heartburn _____
Abdominal pain after eating _____
Bloating _____
Flatulence _____
Coated tongue _____
Constipation _____
Diarrhoea _____
Irritable Bowel Syndrome _____
Catarrh _____
Recurring sore throat _____
Persistent infections _____
Chronic fatigue _____
Muscle weakness _____
Muscle spasm _____
Sudden tiredness _____
Lack of energy _____
Aching joints _____

Restless, twitchy limbs _____
A need for frequent meals _____
Dizziness _____
Palpitations _____
Night sweats _____
Day sweats _____
Excessive thirst _____
Anxiety _____
Irritability _____
Bleeding gums _____
Mouth ulcers _____
Allergies _____
Poor circulation _____
Any other symptoms not included above?

_____ _____
_____ _____
_____ _____
_____ _____

It is important to realize that, in nutritional terms, 30 days is a relatively short period of time and some symptoms may take longer than this to resolve. Any that have occurred recently or that concern you particularly should, of course, be checked out with your doctor.

Important Note
The health tips, food combining guidelines and symptom check list contained in this manual are not prescriptive nor are they an attempt to diagnose or treat any condition. If you are concerned in any way about your health, it is imperative that you consult your own doctor without delay. You should keep your G.P. informed of the progress of any symptoms, of any dietary changes you are making and of any supplement programme you may choose to follow.

Day Two – Starting Afresh

Clean out food cupboards, larder, refrigerator and freezer. Discard anything that is out of date.

Not everything that comes in a packet is bad for you, of course, but it makes healthy common-sense to cut down on packeted ready meals, diet foods, tins and take-aways. Throughout these 30 days, try to reduce or remove processed foods from your diet. Use up any remaining packaged, frozen and tinned meals this week. This is not ideal but, let's face it, food costs money and most people cannot afford to throw it away.

However, if you have already utilized your existing food stores, you may like to begin choosing breakfasts, lunches, dinners and snacks from the recipes provided on pages 133 to 167. If you haven't food combined before, don't concern yourself with the food category headings or worry about not understanding them. Simply choose one protein-based meal, one starch-based meal and one alkaline-forming meal each day. The reasoning behind these recommendations will become clear as you progress through the 30-day programme.

Day Three – Learning About Low-Energy Foods

Food combining is all about enjoyable and healthy eating. Most people are aware that refined, high-fat and high-sugar foods are not so good for us, but there are plenty of supposedly healthy foods that aren't too brilliant either. There are also lots of delicious things which you can include that you probably thought were taboo. Turn to the chapter entitled 'Low-Energy Foods' on page 105 today. Read about some of the unseen snags associated with processed foods and begin to rediscover the pleasures of real food.

Day Four — What are Proteins?

On Days Four and Five we will be learning about Ps and Ss.

P stands for PROTEIN
S stands for STARCH and also for SUGAR

The most important rule of food combining is that *proteins* are not mixed at the same meal as *starches*.

When we talk about protein, we are usually referring to *concentrated proteins* such as meat, fish, eggs and cheese. There is a lot of confusion surrounding protein foods and about how much protein we should eat each day for good health. I am always amused by Harvey Diamond's observation that very little can compare with most people's fear of not getting *enough* protein! The fact is that it's as unhealthy to have too much as it is to have too little.

Go Easy

It is also a fact that most of us consume far too much *concentrated* protein each day for our own good. By inflicting excesses on our children, they also grow up with the idea that the only way to health and strength is to eat large amounts of steak and eggs and to drink gallons of milk, little realizing that they may be risking heart disease, kidney problems, weight problems and all manner of other ills later in life. Harvey Diamond again: 'Kids are the real test. Place a small child in a crib with a rabbit and an apple. If the child eats the rabbit and plays with the apple, I'll buy you a new car.' Children have an innate instinct for what is right to eat as long as their tastes have not been adulterated by someone else's opinions or temptations! They are happy, for example, to eat only one food at a time — which makes them food combining naturals.

How Much is Too Much?

Recommended daily allowances for protein vary around the world, but most experts now agree on between 45g and 55g daily as the amount required to prevent protein deficiency in adults (that's less than two ounces). However, individual needs may differ depending upon body size and activity levels. It certainly doesn't mean that you are risking your health by eating a freshly grilled trout that weighs 170g (6 ounces), but you will be putting a strain on the system if you (a) mix trout with starchy food at the same meal or (b) eat that much protein at every meal every day.

Energy Robbers

Overdoing the protein overburdens the system. Protein is the most complex of all food elements and its digestion and absorption take more time and more energy than any other food. Eating more than is needed simply means that the body has to work all the harder to deal with and eliminate the excess. Doing that *and* mixing it with starch simply compounds the felony.

Apart from stealing energy from you to do this work, excess protein can also increase the toxic overload with which your body has to deal (and as you have seen in the section on weight problems, toxicity can lead to obesity).

Food Combining for Protein Balance

It is easy to forget that a wide variety of foods (vegetables and cereals, for example) contain small amounts of protein (in other words, not concentrated amounts). However, this concentration is too low for them to be labelled 'Proteins'. By keeping the concentrated proteins (the meat, cheese, eggs etc.) within reasonable limits and by eating a diverse range of other foods too, we can consume *healthy* amounts of *healthy* protein. Happily, food combining achieves a natural and cleverly balanced intake of protein foods without fatiguing or forcing the system.

Most Proteins are 'Acid-Forming'

All proteins (except yoghurt and unpasteurized milk*)

---

*Milk is rather a special case since it is alkaline-forming when raw (unpasteurized) but, once pasteurized, its enzyme and protein structure and its calcium content change, making it acid-forming. Since nearly all commercially available milk products are pasteurized, you should treat all milk as acid-forming for the purposes of food combining and use it only very sparingly. You'll find more information in the section on 'Low-Energy Foods' on page 105.

are known as 'acid-forming' foods. Throughout the book, acid-forming foods are marked with a minus sign ('-') and alkaline-forming foods are marked with a plus sign ('+'). However, do not concern yourself with this right now; the terminology is not important. Ideally, only one meal each day should be based on concentrated protein.

Remember that proteins mix well with all kinds of vegetable and salad foods.

Concentrated Proteins are:

- - Meat
- - Poultry
- - Offal
- - Cheese
- - Eggs
- - Fish
- - Shellfish
- - Soya Beans
- - All soya-based products
- + Yoghurt

Day Five — What Are Starches?

Starches are also known as carbohydrates. For the purposes of food combining, starches include oats, rye, barley, rice, wheat, potatoes, all kinds of flour and the starchy foods which are made from them such as pastry, pasta, rice cakes, bread, biscuits, crackers, and breakfast cereals etc. (See also Food Lists page 125.) But I'm not suggesting that, to food combine successfully, you need to chew your way through the kind of roughage described by Frank Muir, the British writer, broadcaster and renowned wit: 'Some breakfast food manufacturer hit upon the simple notion of emptying out the leavings of carthorse nosebags, adding a few other things like unconsumed portions of chicken layers' mash and the sweepings of racing stables, packing the mixture in little bags and selling them in health food shops.'

Sweetenings and sugary foods are also listed with starches and *are therefore not happy when mixed with proteins*. (See Food Lists, page 125.)

Remember that all starches mix well with all kinds of vegetable and salad foods.

Brown is Best

Food Combining In 30 Days concentrates on the use of what are known as 'complex carbohydrates'; i.e. whole oats, whole rye, wholewheat bread, brown pasta etc. which make great body fuels and sustain our appetites so that we feel fuller for longer. When food combining, it's recommended that one meal per day is starch-based. For example, you might choose a jacket potato with salad, wholewheat pasta and mixed vegetables, stir-fry brown rice, wholegrain bread with avocado or one of the less familiar grains like couscous, quinoa, millet or buckwheat.

Most Starches are 'Acid-Forming'

Apart from alkaline-forming millet, all grains are classed as acid-forming. This does not, however, mean that they are bad for us. On the contrary; wholegrains play an essential role in providing one of the kinds of dietary fibre needed to keep the digestive tract (and particularly the bowel) healthy. Wholegrains also help to maintain stable blood glucose levels and balanced cholesterol and blood pressure. Diets that lack dietary fibre and are rich in refined carbohydrates such as white flour products and lots of sugary foods are known to encourage diverticula disease, bowel cancer, constipation, haemorrhoids (piles), appendicitis, hypertension (high blood pressure) and heart disease.

> The most important rule of food combining is that the two food groups of *proteins* and *starches* are not mixed together at the same meal.

Why Not?

Despite the insistence of some experts, the human body is not designed to (efficiently) digest more than one concentrated food at a time. Concentrated foods are those that contain a high concentration of either protein or starch. Put simply, any food that is not a vegetable or a fruit is *concentrated*. Our forebears would not have understood the concept of the mixed meal where lots of different food groups are collected together and eaten at the same time. Mankind's early ancestors were frugivorous (fruit eating). When we evolved into omnivores, concentrated proteins – such as wild boar – would have been eaten alone, not squashed together with breadcrumbs, made into burgers and put into a bun or served with French fries and apple turnover. Your overtaxed, under-energized system may deal with mixed foods after a fashion and because there may be no immediate minus points, no sudden or short-term risk to life, such concentrated combinations are not perceived as dangerous.

Some people may mix all manner of foods in countless combinations and appear to live long, healthy lives. For those with obdurate obesity and less than perfect health, however, regular consumption of bread with cheese, cereal with milk, eggs with toast or meat with potatoes leads to fatigue and persistently poor health.

Before you panic into wondering what else is left to eat, let me assure you that there is a wide and wonderful variety. Anyway, no one is suggesting that you give up these foods — simply that you eat them in the right combinations.

Simple Example:

Say you were thinking of having fish with brown rice and vegetables for lunch. Split the Ps from the Ss by eating fish (protein) with salad in the middle of the day and enjoying brown rice (starch) with vegetables for your evening meal,

OR

Instead of chicken with potatoes, have a jacket spud (starch) with mushrooms and a side salad for lunch, leaving the chicken (protein) to serve with vegetables that evening.

Why the Mix Matters

For those who enjoy perfect health, tiptop energy and have no weight problems, eating proteins and starches together may appear to be problem-free. But for many others, doing so causes considerable discomfort.

Proteins and starches are treated entirely differently by the digestion. For the starchy potatoes, rice, pasta, oats and other grains, breakdown begins at the moment you start to chew the food. The saliva contains enzymes which, with the help of the teeth, smash the starch into smaller, more manageable and more easily assimilated components. When starchy foods disappear down the hatch to the stomach, the enzymes from the saliva stay active for at least another half an hour — at which time acids are produced to help continue the process.

Proteins such as meat, poultry, fish, eggs and cheese need to be chewed thoroughly, of course, but their actual digestion doesn't begin until they are set upon by the stomach acids (which, as you may recall, the starches prefer to avoid for a while in the initial proceedings but which proteins need as soon as they arrive).

Now picture what can happen when you mix your Ps and Ss:

The proteins are shouting for stomach acids to be served and the starches are saying 'Hang on a minute, we're not ready yet'. One way or the other, one *or* the other (or both) won't be digested properly. Result? Drained energy, loss of nourishment, gas, bloating, flatulence, unpleasant odours, discomfort and pain — which can sometimes be very severe indeed.

I have heard one or two people say that careful combining is unimportant and that the body will cope. My experience with patients suggests the absolute opposite. The symptoms of indigestion are unpleasant enough, but are perhaps not taken seriously because they are not usually perceived to be life threatening.

(Any unusual or dogged discomfort, pain, bleeding, sickness, nausea or altered bowel movements should, in fact, be investigated at once.) Even when no organic disorder can be found, persistent indigestion should be taken as a clear signal by the sufferer that all is not well.

Poor digestion = poor absorption = loss of vital nutrients = compromised immunity = reduced ability to fight infections = increased risk of degenerative disease etc. None of this will happen overnight but, little by little, the system finds it harder to cope. Simple alterations to the basic diet could have prevented problems occurring in the first place.

Classic Case History

An example of this is the patient who had suffered with indigestion for so many years that he carried antacid tablets in every jacket, coat and trouser pocket – even in the glove compartment of his car. When he could tolerate the pain no longer, he visited his G.P. who tried several different medicines (all to no avail). The patient was then referred to a specialist and put through the mill of myriad hospital tests and examinations from barium meal X-rays to gastroscopes (twice) and coloscopy. Nothing untoward could be found.

I gave the man a copy of *The Food Combining Diet*. In six weeks, he reported that he had suffered no indigestion whatsoever, his irritable bowel stopped being irritable and he had 'tons of energy'. All remaining antacid tablets had been consigned directly to the sewers! The doctor was pleased, amazed and puzzled. The patient was thrilled.

Day Six –
Think Positively About Eating Well

If there seems to be an initial drawback to becoming a food combiner, it is the mistaken belief that the loss of certain (unhealthy) food combinations will make the programme difficult to follow. Definitely and absolutely not true. Whilst it is necessary to say goodbye to some familiar mixes such as meat with potatoes, fish and chips or bread and cheese, no-one is, for a moment, suggesting that you have to give up these foods but simply that you will eat them in different combinations.

Anyone who understands a little basic school chemistry will know that acids are cancelled out by alkalis. As explained in the section on proteins and starches, mixing a food that requires acid conditions for digestion (protein) with one that needs an alkaline medium (starch) will create a neutral environment (neither acid nor alkaline) in which nothing will be digested properly. So it makes real sense not to mix foods that fight.

A great favourite for some people is shepherd's pie and it can be difficult to visualize life without mince and mashed potato until you've tried the food combiners' version called 'Shepherd's Parsnips'. Instead of a potato topping, use mashed, buttered parsnips. It's delicious.

In our house, we still enjoy fish and chips but we don't have them at the same meal. Grilled mackerel with salad, whitebait with stir-fried vegetables, poached salmon with broccoli, fresh trout shallow fried in olive oil — all these are favourite (and filling) fish dishes with not a chip in sight.

When it comes to chips, many people still believe that frying them in polyunsaturated oil is healthier than using lard or dripping. Well, it isn't — because poly oils are horribly unstable at temperature. When they're heated and reheated they become a toxic health hazard. Anyhow, there's no need to deep-fry anything. Make healthy chips or scallops by cooking your sliced potatoes in a couple of tablespoons of extra virgin olive oil. Turn them a couple of times during cooking (15—20 minutes) and sprinkle with a little lo-salt or sea salt before serving. Everyone I know who has tried this method so far says that they prefer the end result to the chips they used to have! The full recipe is on page 157.

Forego the melted cheese on your jacket potato and substitute a knob of butter, some mashed avocado, fresh coleslaw or a dollop of hummus.

Enjoy your pasta with shredded, stir-fried vegetables or garlic, herb or butter sauce instead of cheese.

If cheese is your fancy, a chunk of Cheddar or Brie goes brilliantly with sticks of fresh, crispy celery.

Sandwiches are simple. Avoid protein fillings such as egg, cheese, tuna or chicken and opt for tomato, cucumber, lettuce, watercress, grated carrot, avocado, sliced red or green peppers, carob spread, sprouted seeds and fresh herbs in any combination. Or put your fried potato (above) in-between two slices of wholegrain bread for a really up-market chip butty.

As you can see from the recipes on pages 133—167, *Food Combining In 30 Days* contains plenty of tasty recipe ideas for you to choose from and there are lots more in *The Food Combining Diet*. Many of the books in the Recommended Reading section on page 171 contain further mouthwatering recipes.

Day Seven – Easy Exercise

To make the most of your new healthy eating programme, you must exercise – and by exercise, I mean the aerobic variety. Humans are 'aerobians' – they live on free oxygen from the air. Aerobic is the term now used to mean exercise with oxygen, the kind of movement that increases your heart and pulse rates, makes you breathe more quickly and more deeply and makes you sweat! What's so wonderful about aerobic exercise – apart from the fact that it strengthens your heart and helps protect you from heart attacks – is the fact that everyone who can put one foot in front of the other can do it.

Now this does not mean that you have to run a marathon every day before breakfast, jog the tarmac until you drop or workout to oblivion. One of the biggest barriers to exercise is surely the feeling that you are being forced into something you don't want, don't like, haven't the time for or which is just plain unsuitable for your needs. It's the same with exercise as it is with food – moderation and enjoyment are the key words to keep in mind.

One of the greatest dangers associated with exercise is doing too much. After any kind of 'workout', whether it's running, rebounding, brisk walking, gym training or half an hour in front of your favourite video, you should feel pleasantly puffed and revitalized, not exhausted and drained.

Exercise in the fresh air is particularly beneficial because not only are you benefiting from negatively charged ions in the atmosphere (most buildings are polluted with positive ions from electrical equipment and man-made materials), but also your skin is seeing daylight. Even on an overcast day, there are enough of the sun's rays permeating the cloud to activate vitamin D production via the skin. Vitamin D is essential for calcium absorption and utilization and is now being studied as a likely anti-cancer vitamin; which just goes to show that too little exposure to sunlight may be as foolish as too much!

Because exercise outside is good for you, that doesn't mean that exercise taken indoors is not. Not everyone has access to uncrowded countryside or pollution-free parks and sometimes and in some areas, sad to say, it simply isn't safe to go out alone. Exercising at home can be relaxing and fun. There are plenty of excellent fitness videos around to choose from; my personal favourite is the Josh Salzmann *Bodyfit* Video (by Pickwick), which is a great accompaniment to his *Bodyfit* book (Thorsons).

Using a rebounder (a kind of firm mini-trampoline) is a wonderful way of exercising; even if you haven't exercised for years, just a few minutes a day will be of enormous benefit. If you can build up to fifteen to twenty minutes on a rebounder, this is said to be as beneficial as pounding hard pavements for an hour – and you don't need special clothing or high ceilings. I have a rebounder which I use indoors during the winter and outdoors in the garden during the fine weather. Rebounding is better for your bone structure than jogging and is especially useful for anyone who finds that running or jogging causes pain. It tones and strengthens every cell in the body, helps shed dead skin cells and detoxifies the system. Information on where to find one is in the Resources section on page 174.

If videos aren't your scene and you don't have room for a rebounder, there are still plenty of options: cycling, dancing, swimming, keep fit and sensible weight training are all beneficial types of exercise.

Isotonics, for example, is a special type of weight, strength and resistance training which builds up muscle mass, which in turn raises the body's metabolic rate and therefore helps you to burn off calories – and lose weight – more quickly. Increasing muscle mass also *decreases* the risk of developing diabetes, for it reduces the amount of insulin required to take glucose from the blood into the tissues, where it is needed for energy; and adult diabetes is often triggered by the body 'running out' of insulin.

Isotonic exercise increases bone density (thereby protecting against osteoporosis) and research suggests that it may even help sufferers from rheumatoid arthritis. Any kind of weight or strength training is best learnt from a professional, but once learnt the good results should encourage you to keep it up.

Begin Slowly

Today, Day Seven of your programme, make a resolution to increase your activity levels by taking the stairs and leaving the lift alone, by walking to the next tube or bus stop rather than the one nearest home and by stretching your legs in your lunch break. None of this can really be called aerobic exercise (unless your walk is a brisk one of over a mile) but it is still valuable. If you are unused to exercising regularly, it's really important to begin slowly and work your way towards increased activity levels week by week. Launching yourself unprepared into vigorous exertion can lead to stress, strain and injury. So, start off gently and increase your fitness levels gradually; we'll learn more about exercise on Day Twenty-One.

Important Notes

1 *Before beginning any new exercise programme, ask for specialist assistance from a qualified fitness expert, aerobics teacher, swimming coach or gym instructor. If you are unsure about whether or not a particular exercise routine is compatible with your present health status, if you have an existing health problem and are receiving medication, then ask your practitioner for advice prior to commencing any programme.*

2 *If you feel pain or discomfort when exercising, then STOP IMMEDIATELY.*

3 *If you exercise particularly strenuously on a particular day and feel tired the next day, then rest and recover before exercising again.*

Overview

What a great week. You've taken a good look at your present state of health; really thinking about any physical symptoms and what your body is trying to tell you leads to greater body awareness and encourages you to do something about it. In reorganizing your food stores and learning about low-energy eating habits you have made your kitchen a source of truly nutritious and health-giving foods. You have taken your first food combining steps. To complete your first seven days you have begun to increase your activity levels. Keep up the good work throughout this coming week!

Week 2 (Days 8–14)

Practically Food Combining

❧

In treating a patient, let your first thought be to
strengthen his vitality.

Rhazes (Ar-Razi; 850–923),
Persian physician and philosopher

Aims for the Week

This week you will encounter the concept of acid-forming
and alkaline-forming foods; but needn't worry about
understanding it yet. From Day Nine you'll introduce
more fresh fruit into your diet and start to follow the fruit
rule. Enjoying the versatile 'mix-with-anything' foods will
become a daily delight. Questioning your digestion will
lead to greater body awareness and healthier eating
habits. You'll begin to cut down a little on your caffeine
intake and to drink more water. The Deep Breathing
Exercises on Day Fourteen will show you how correct
breathing can detoxify your system — and help you to
relax!

Day Eight –
Acid-Forming and Alkaline-Forming Foods

At first, this area of food combining may seem a little confusing. But it really isn't. When I first began to study food combining, it was the one area which – initially – confused me too. Even now, I receive letters from people who have struggled with early food combining books and cannot grasp the terminology.

Then, a colleague of mine who is a renowned food combining expert pointed out to me that, first of all, it wasn't really necessary to understand the chemistry of acid/alkaline-forming foods and, second of all, if the other food combining guidelines were followed, the acid/alkaline instalment would become clear. I followed his advice and, joy of joys, food combining fell into place.

Since then, I have learned as much as possible about – and become fascinated by – this all-important aspect of eating for optimum health. In fact, achieving the right balance of 'acid' and 'alkaline' foods, although a particular part of the food combining programme, is also fundamental to healthy eating in general and so is important for everyone, not just for food combiners.

The Chemistry Connection

The acidity or alkalinity of any substance is measured by its 'pH'. Zero pH is very acid, a pH of 14 is very alkaline. The pH of water is 7 which indicates neutral (in other words, neither acid nor alkaline). Put another way, figures over 7 indicate alkaline, figures below 7 (beer has a pH of 4.5) mean acid. Blood is maintained at a precarious alkaline constant of between 7.35 and 7.45 pH; anything more than the tiniest deviation either way can result in illness and death. So, keeping these levels in balance is vital to the body's survival. Whilst the body has a natural mechanism for keeping the acid/alkali levels in check, you can help a great deal by contributing the right foods.

Whether or not a food has an alkaline-forming (alkalizing) or acid-forming effect upon the body is determined by what happens to it during digestion and what kind of mineral 'ash' is left behind after the food has been metabolized. Apart from the aforementioned alcoholic beverage, acid-forming foods include meat, poultry, fish, grains and pulses which, after digestion and metabolism, leave behind deposits of chlorine and sulphur. Sulphur is one of the gases responsible for odorous flatulence! Alkaline-forming foods (fresh fruits, vegetables and salads) are broken down into residues of different minerals including calcium, magnesium and potassium. To maintain good health, we need more of the mineral deposits from alkaline-forming foods than we do from the acid-forming ones. Unfortunately, for many people, the reverse applies; food combining is a great way to redress the balance.

For the purposes of simple food combining, there is really no need to lose any sleep over trying to comprehend the chemistry behind all of this.

Just remember that:

Acid ash and alkali ash have different functions
We need both kinds for good health
Most of us need to increase on the alkaline-forming kind

Almost without thinking, it's easy to take on board too many acid-forming energy sappers. Toast and cereal for breakfast, meat, cheese or egg sandwiches for lunch and meat, poultry or fish for dinner would make up three very acid-forming meals. There is nothing wrong with any of those foods in moderation, of course. Indeed, in reasonable quantities, they are positively beneficial.

However, overdose on them and they can be the cause of sour stomachs, poor digestion, body odour, bad breath, headaches, irritability and ulcers! And more so if the intake of fresh fruits, vegetables and salads is low or non-existent. Too many late nights, chronic fatigue, negative stress, anxiety, fear, worry, cigarettes and excess alcohol will only add to the acid overload.

Picture alkalizing foods as acid-buffers and it's easy to see what an important job they have in neutralizing excess acids and in cleansing and invigorating (or vitalizing) the blood and tissues. In fact, I tend to think of alkalizing and vitalizing as much the same thing. Fresh, alkaline-forming foods are vital foods, rich in minerals, which assist in the rebuilding and repair of blood, bone, tissue and nerves. They help to support the elimination processes and assist in the breakdown and eviction of dead cells and other unwanted wastes.

Food combining achieves the 'just right' balance of alkaline-forming and acid-forming foods by recommending a daily intake of:

One protein-based meal with vegetables or salad
One starch-based meal with vegetables or salad
One completely alkaline-forming salad, vegetable or fruit meal

It also helps to remember that:

Foods that take longer to digest (i.e. proteins and
  starches) tend to be acid-forming
Foods that are digested quickly (i.e. fruit, salads and
  vegetables) are mostly alkaline-forming

However, if you find it isn't possible to keep to the
one alkaline, one starch, one protein meal per day
recommendation, it is, in fact, o.k. to vary this theme
by having:

Two starch and one alkaline
or
Two alkaline and one starch
or
One protein and two alkaline
or even
Two starch and one protein

meals per day.

As long as you can aim for a total of seven protein
meals, seven starch meals and seven alkaline meals each
week, the combination is flexible. We live in an often
uncompromising world where there isn't always the
time — or even the inclination — to get everything
absolutely right. Being a pedantic perfectionist can also
be boring, exhausting and stressful, not just for you but
for everyone around you, too.

How to Recognize an Over-Acid System

Just as it isn't necessary to understand the 'mechanics' of acid/alkali stability, you don't need a Masters degree in chemistry to tell you if it's off balance. Because we tend to overeat sugary foods and proteins, it's easy to reach acid saturation. Waking up feeling drugged with a furred or tacky tongue, a sour taste and evil breath are likely signs that your blood and tissues are acid-logged! (The deep breathing exercises which you begin on Day Thirteen are believed by many experts to be alkalizing – which is why it's a good idea to practise them first thing in the morning as well as last thing at night.)

For most people, it's harder to become *over-alkalized* since fruits and vegetables tend to be lower on their list of individual preferences or priorities. But it *is* possible if *too many* of your meals are salads, vegetables or fruit only and your diet is not balanced with a sensible intake of proteins and starches.

In the main, however, it makes sense to:

Increase the intake of fresh vegetables and salads either as meals on their own or mixed with proteins or starches.
Increase the intake of fresh fruit either as starters or between-meal snacks.

A Basic List of Alkaline-Forming Foods
- Almonds
- Brazil nuts
- All kinds of seeds including caraway, celery, dill,

fennel, fenugreek, linseeds, poppy seeds, pumpkin, sesame and sunflower seeds
- Millet — the only alkaline-forming grain
- Any vegetables (the only exception is acid-forming asparagus)
- All fruits
- All salad foods (tomatoes are alkaline-forming when raw but become acid-forming once they are cooked)
- All herbs

Throughout the book, you will see that acid-forming foods are marked with a minus sign ('-') and alkaline-forming foods are marked with a plus ('+').

Day Nine — The Fruit Rule

Fruit is, without doubt, one of the most beneficial nutrient and energy sources. Its high water content, together with its rich stores of vitamins, minerals and natural sugars, make it one of the most nourishing foods. It should become a frequent and fundamental part of your food combining diet but eat it separately from proteins and starches.

I have often heard patients say that they *would* eat more fruit if only it didn't disagree with them. They lay the blame for any pain, bloating or irritable bowel on the fruit itself and rarely consider the crazy combination in which it was probably eaten.

It is a common habit to grab a lunchtime sandwich and follow it immediately with an apple. It is also common to spend the afternoon doubled up with stomach cramp or heartburn as a direct result. A fruit salad dessert shoved swiftly down after a mingled main course can cause similar grief. And it's no wonder.

Fruit likes a speedy passage through the stomach but other foods, like proteins and starches, take much longer. When eaten alone, fruit has free access to the next port of call in the digestive system, the small intestine, where it gives up its vital nutrient-packed energy. Fruit is not digested in the stomach and hates being mixed with other foods. If forced to be so, the mixture will rot, ferment, produce gas and become instantly acid-forming.

Dr Hay believed that it was acceptable to mix *certain* fruits with protein foods and on this point he and I would doubtless have had lively discussions. Dr Herbert Shelton, on the other hand, regarded by most practitioners as *the* food combining guru, would not have agreed with Dr Hay either. If you read other food combining books, you will find some that mix acid fruits with protein and sweet ripe fruits with starch. However, I have found this idea particularly confusing and I do know that it is one of the major reasons why food combining has, in the past, been seen as difficult to follow. Once fruit is separated from other foods and eaten separately, the whole system is simplified.

Protein requires three to four hours in the stomach chamber and fruit only fifteen to twenty minutes. If the two are chewed up and mixed together, how can they then be separated for efficient digestion?

My own preference for eating fruit on an empty stomach is further supported by my experience and success in treating digestive disorders. Removing or 'rescheduling' the fruit component of a main meal has, in very many cases, cancelled the patient's digestive discomfort completely without any other intervention. A much better option than reaching for the bicarbonate of soda or indigestion tablets!

So think of fruit as the Greta Garbo of food combining. It prefers to be alone.

Always follow the fruit rules:

Eat two or three pieces of fruit every day.　　·
but
Eat it on an empty stomach.
that is
Either before a meal (and leave a gap of 15 to 20 minutes between courses).
or
As a between-meal snack.
or
As a meal on its own, for example a delicious fruit-only breakfast.

There is no restriction on quantity — eat as much as you like at one sitting to satisfy your hunger.

These fruit combinations make tasty, filling and satisfying breakfasts or snacks:

- apple, pineapple, papaya, grapes and figs
- apple, pear and raisins
- mango, papaya, peach and nectarine
- grapefruit, apple and satsuma
- grapes, kiwi fruit and pineapple

See the Recipe section on page 159 for more tempting ways of serving fruit.

NB Melons are digested even more quickly than other fruits and so should be eaten entirely separately from everything else including other fruit. If you choose melon as a starter, leave about 15 minutes between courses.

Instant Energy

The concentrated sugars in fruit are an easily absorbed form called fructose. Unlike sucrose (ordinary brown or white table sugar is sucrose), which needs the hormone insulin to break it down into simple sugars before it can be absorbed, fructose is taken straight into the body's storage system without putting unnecessary strain on the pancreas or other endocrine glands.

Good for Hypoglycaemics

For some people, especially recovering hypoglycaemics (see Day Twenty-Two), it helps to stagger the morning fruit intake, so as to maintain blood sugar at a fairly constant level. If you have eaten an apple and some grapes for breakfast, for example, then it's a good idea to have pineapple and kiwi or a couple of bananas at, say, 10.30 or 11.00 a.m. Bananas are particularly comforting and useful if you are peckish.

Cooked and Canned Fruits

Canned and stewed fruits are not generally recommended as they no longer contain the same nourishment as the fresh version. Fruit has a fragile nature; heating and processing denature the nutrients so that it becomes acid-forming instead of alkaline-forming. All food combining experts, including Dr Hay, Dr Shelton and Harvey and Marilyn Diamond, agree that cooked fruits contain no cleansing qualities. That is not to say they are banned completely but that they should be taken only occasionally and in small quantities. Similarly, canned fruit in natural juices makes a useful emergency cupboard store but should not be relied upon as the only fruit supply.

Fruit Juices

Freshly prepared juice is a wonderful way to start the day. If you have your own juicing machine, you can prepare a delicious variety of different concoctions. If not, it's best to buy additive-free, non-carbonated juices in glass bottles. Always remember that juices oxidize (degenerate) very quickly indeed once they are extracted from the fruit so, as soon as they are prepared, consume them IMMEDIATELY. Don't wait even for a minute or two before you drink them. This applies particularly in the case of juice prepared using juicing machines. They are efficient and produce excellent results but all goodness will be lost in seconds if the juice is attacked by oxygen. Notice how quickly an apple turns brown once the peel has been removed? Well, it's the same with juices.

As with fresh fruit, remember that juices should be consumed only on an empty stomach!

WAKE UP TO JUICES

One of the best ways of starting the day is to prepare fresh juice first thing before you disappear into the bathroom and to eat a breakfast of whole fruit after you have bathed and dressed. This method of fruit consumption is especially cleansing, invigorating and energizing – and a terrific way to get the inner workings working!

ORANGE JUICE

The media image of fresh orange juice for breakfast has become so synonymous with good health that suggesting it could be a mistake is likely to bring forth howls of protest. Unfortunately, however, cartoned and bottled orange juice is very often pasteurized which, like milk pasteurization, alters the nutritional value of the juice. In addition, some brands are not as fresh as they are promoted to be and may contain additional acids, additives, sugar and, sometimes, pulpwash, produced by soaking the fruit skins in water. These 'appendages' are not usually declared even on labels that display the words 'fresh', 'pure' or 'real' juice. In addition, orange juice is notorious for causing headaches and exacerbating arthritic pain, joint stiffness and indigestion.

Once the orange has been cut from its parent plant, the vitamin C content begins to diminish. It reduces even further when the juice is extracted from the fruit and exposed to heat, light and air. If you are hooked on orange juice, my advice would be to prepare your own at home from real oranges or to make sure that you buy unadulterated, freshly squeezed juice (you should be able to see bits of fruit in the juice).

CHEW YOUR JUICES

The famous American food combining expert, Wayne Pickering, who also believes that fruit should be eaten separately from other foods, advises that we should chew our liquids and drink our solid foods. As so much digestion begins in the mouth, this makes complete sense. Liquids should not be gulped, but consumed slowly and sloshed around in the mouth before swallowing. Solid foods should be chewed so thoroughly that they are in a semi-liquid form before they are swallowed. The more work done by the teeth and the saliva, the less work for the stomach and other digestive organs.

Here are some of my favourite juice combinations:

- Apple, pear and kiwi
- Apple, grape and raw beetroot (make sure you wear an apron!)
- Carrot and apple
- Apple and celery
- Pineapple and kiwi
- Pineapple, mango and papaya
- Orange and grapefruit
- Blackcurrant, kiwi and orange
- Papaya and peach (or nectarine)

NB Bananas do not juice well, but can be mashed separately and mixed in with other juices using a fork or whisk. And remember, melon juice is best drunk on its own.

Waiting Timetable

It is helpful to know how long you should wait after eating a meal before you can reintroduce fruit or fruit juice. As explained above, fruit and its juices should be taken on an empty stomach; but how long does it take for the stomach to become empty? This table is a useful guide.

Meal type	Waiting time
After a fruit-only meal	Whenever suits you
After a salad or vegetable-only meal	Wait 1 hour
After a starch-based meal	Wait 3 hours
After a protein-based meal of cheese, eggs, yoghurt or soya i.e. non-flesh food	Wait 3 hours
After a protein-based meal of flesh food	Wait 4 hours
After any meal that is not properly combined	Wait 6 hours

You'll find a comprehensive list of fruits to choose from, whether for eating whole or for juicing, on pages 126–127.

Day Ten – The 'Mix With Anything' Foods

So far, we have heard about the foods that don't mix well with others. For example, proteins don't like being with starches; fruits prefer to be alone. But there are lots of delicious foods which, because they are 'neutral' (i.e. not heavily concentrated proteins or starches), will mix happily with anything.

You will notice that, in the recipes starting on page 133, vegetables, salads, seeds, fats, oils, herbs and spices turn up in protein *and* starch menus. Well, this is because they are versatile mixers, useful additions to any starch-based or protein-based meal. They can also be combined with each other or eaten separately; you'll find helpful lists of some of these versatile foods in the Food Lists section on page 125, and the mix-and-match Easy Reference Chart on page 131 is very useful for displaying in the kitchen or referring to with your shopping list, so make a copy of it now to keep with you.

Day Eleven — Drink More Water

Drink more water (preferably filtered). My recommended *minimum* intake is TWO PINTS OF WATER per day (just over one litre, also translated as four tumblers or six average-sized glasses) in addition to other drinks. Try to drink between meals or before meals but avoid copious quantities of fluid with food, apart from a small amount which may be needed to take any supplements or medication. Overflowing the fluids at meal times simply makes food too dilute; it then passes much too speedily through the system resulting in incomplete digestion.

A special tip to help increase your water intake, that I have recommended to patients for many years, is to have a glass of water near you and to sip at it throughout the day. It will quickly empty and require refilling. Drink a glass of water first thing in the morning before breakfast and another while you are preparing or waiting for lunch and dinner. Small bottles of water are useful for popping into the door pocket or seat pouch in your car or carrying in your bag.

Day Twelve – Cutting Down the Caffeine

How much tea and coffee do you drink? If it's more than four cups (total) per day, try to cut down if you can – and watch your intake of other caffeine-rich drinks such as cola and hot chocolate. There's no need to give up good-quality tea and coffee since a sensible and moderate amount can be enjoyable and, studies show, may even offer some health benefits. An excess of poor-quality coffee and tea, on the other hand, appears to aggravate some symptoms including insomnia, anxiety, palpitations, headaches and fatigue.

The better brands are usually naturally lower in caffeine. Going for decaffeinated may seem like a good idea but you are avoiding only one of many chemicals by doing so (and some brands actually introduce extra chemicals in the decaffeination process). Useful alternatives for those trying to unhook themselves from caffeine (it is a drug, after all) include herbal or fruit teas, grain-based coffee substitutes, carob drinks, fresh juices and water. For more information on fruit juices, see pages 62–65. For top-quality teas and coffee which are naturally low in caffeine or caffeine-free, see Resources on page 176.

Day Thirteen — Improving Your Digestion

Most of us eat our food far too quickly — often without even realizing the torture our digestive systems are going through. Today, answer the questions in this quiz and, when you have completed it, check your 'digestibility' scores.

Do you go without food all day and
then eat a large meal in the evening?   YES/NO

Do you miss breakfast more than once a
week?   YES/NO

Do you drink more than a small glass or
cup of liquid with meals?   YES/NO

Do you eat fruit as a dessert?   YES/NO

Do you always drink tea or coffee
immediately after a meal?   YES/NO

Do you always get up to clear the table
or to go back to work as soon as you
have finished eating?   YES/NO

Do you drink fruit juice with meals?   YES/NO

Do you always finish your meal before
everyone else?   YES/NO

Do you enjoy lots of spicy foods?   YES/NO

Do you enjoy lots of chilled drinks and
ice cream?   YES/NO

Are you overweight?   YES/NO

Do you eat take-away or packeted ready
meals more than once a week?   YES/NO

Do you take indigestion remedies more
than three times a year?   YES/NO

Do you eat out in restaurants more than
once a week?   YES/NO

Is eating out an inevitable part of your
job?   YES/NO

Do you eat one course immediately after
another without more than a couple of
minutes in-between?   YES/NO

Do you eat reheated food more than
once a week?   YES/NO

Do you mix proteins and starches at the
same meal?   YES/NO

Do you feel stressed when you eat?   YES/NO

Are you usually rushed and hurried?   YES/NO

If you answered 'yes' to more than three of these
questions, then the chances are your digestion is under
significant strain.

To reduce the burden, introduce as many of the
following tips as possible. Your system will function
more efficiently and you'll begin to absorb and make
use of the food you are eating.

- Always have breakfast – or if you are not a
  breakfast person, enjoy a light meal of fresh fruit
  and fruit juices as soon as you can in the
  morning.
- If you feel hungry, eat something. Don't put up
  with hunger pangs just because it isn't a
  regulation meal time. A piece of fresh fruit
  makes a great snack.
- Avoid drinking large quantities of fluid with food.
  A small glass of wine before a meal or sufficient
  liquid to swallow medication or supplements is
  fine.
- Drink plenty of water between meals.
- Keep all fruits and fruit juices separate from
  proteins and starches.

- Never eat 'on the run'.
- Sit down to your meals, chew your food thoroughly and remain seated for ten minutes after you have finished eating.
- Wash all fruits and vegetables before use; unwashed fruit may carry germs or pesticide residues which can upset the digestion.
- Very cold or very hot foods can disturb the digestion so take care and have them only occasionally.
- Enjoy your tea and coffee but drink them between meals, not immediately after food: they can disturb digestion.
- Allow time between courses. Don't rush from starter to main course to sweet, as if it were a relay race.
- Don't rely on reheats. Reheated foods should be for emergencies only. In addition, reheating destroys nutrients.
- Don't eat if you are very anxious, stressed or in a hurry. If you are really short on time, sit down and satisfy your immediate hunger with a piece of fresh fruit (which takes less time to eat and is digested more efficiently).
- Eating little and often is better than going for long periods without food and then filling up with an enormous meal. Even the most nourishing of foods will not be digested properly if you overload the system.
- Avoid rich meals and keep food simple. When eating out, hold the heavy sauces and deep-fried food and opt instead for lighter dishes with salad or vegetables.

- Be sensible about take-aways and ready meals. They are usually high in fat, sugar and additives. Check the menu for healthier alternatives or buy the basic ingredients and prepare the meal yourself from scratch. A piece of grilled or poached fish with salad can be ready in five minutes — far less time than it takes to queue for a take-away or to microwave a frozen dinner.
- Choose food that is as close to its natural, unprocessed state as possible. Really fresh produce is always going to be a better bet than something out of a can.
- Include plenty of variety in your diet and don't go to extremes.
- Don't plough your way through a meal which you don't particularly like just because you think it's healthy.
- Don't mix proteins and starches at the same meal. If you separate them, you won't need indigestion remedies!

Day Fourteen — Exercise Your Insides

I hope that, since Day Seven, you've been gradually increasing the amount of aerobic activity in your routine, whether it's walking, rebounding, cycling, swimming or any other favourite type of exercise. Add to your fitness programme from today by introducing a special breathing exercise.

Deep breathing:

- Relaxes and de-stresses the system

- Improves the transport of oxygen and other nutrients around the body
- Exercises internal organs
- Detoxifies the system
- Improves energy during the day
- Encourages sound sleep at night
- Improves the circulation.

Deep breathing exercises are an essential part of any exercise programme. For those who are disabled or have limited movement, they are even more important.

Follow these basic breathing exercises first thing in the morning (before you get out of bed) and at night (while you are waiting to go to sleep). They'll take only a few minutes in total. In fact, many people tell me that the night exercises are so relaxing that they often fall asleep before they have finished them!

The Twice Daily Breathing Exercise

1 Lie on your back with one pillow supporting your head and neck.
2 Before you begin, be certain that you are comfortable, relaxed and warm enough. Deliberately tense and relax your toes, legs, buttocks, shoulders, arms, hands (make a fist and let go), neck, jaw and eyes.
3 Then exhale gently and completely with a big sigh.
4 Begin to breathe in, so that your abdomen extends and the lower ribs expand . . . keep on breathing in so that air fills your chest . . . hold for one second.

5 Then exhale very slowly and very gently.

6 Before taking in the second full breath, hold for a count of two.

7 Breathe in and out again following the same pattern. Do this a further nine times.

8 During the exercises, keep the mouth gently closed and breathe in and out through the nose.

9 Avoid strain and breathe only to comfortable limits.

10 Breathe away all darkness, gloom, anger, resentment, impatience and distress. Breathe in tranquillity, serenity, stillness and comfort into your whole being.

11 When you have completed your morning exercises, breathe normally for two minutes before getting out of bed. Deep breathing can lower the blood pressure and if you are new to this type of exercise, getting up too quickly may make you feel slightly dizzy.

Important Note
If you have a heart condition or blood pressure disorder, check with your G.P. before doing these exercises.

Overview

This week, you have become familiar with the concept of acid and alkaline-forming foods. You have introduced the fruit rule, and have begun to eat more fruit and to drink delicious fresh juices. Reading about the neutral 'mix with anything' foods has increased your understanding of food combining. You have taken steps to improve your digestion, to cut down on coffee and tea and to drink more water. By learning to breathe more deeply you will begin to sleep more soundly and will feel more relaxed. Over the next two weeks, you'll continue to put all these healthy habits into practice.

Week 3 (Days 15–21)

Cleansing and Nurturing

⟡

> Nature, time and patience are the three great physicians.
>
> *Bulgarian proverb*

Aims For The Week

This week you will discover how to cleanse and detoxify the system and how to ensure that you are looking after your digestion. On Day Eighteen you'll have a chance to review the food combining rules concerning proteins and starches. You'll check that you are eating enough fruit and will increase the overall quality of your food intake. On Day Twenty-One you'll find helpful hints to add to your gentle exercise programme.

Days Fifteen and Sixteen – The Two-Day Detox Programme

Whatever your normal eating habits, it can be very beneficial to add a regular inner-cleansing routine to your lifestyle. Over Days Fifteen and Sixteen you will be introduced to The Two-Day Detox Programme, which is something you can return to every couple of weeks, or once a month if that's more convenient. For these two days, take a rest from the food lists which you have been using and adopt the 'Two-Day Detox', which is based on the alkaline-forming foods you were reading about on Day Eight. This kind of cleansing routine is terrific anytime you are feeling run down, under par, overtired or stressed or are suffering the after-effects of too many late nights or over-indulgences. Detox dieting is enjoyable, easy to do and won't leave you feeling hungry. And it's full of nutrient-packed alkaline-forming foods, which are also a fundamental part of food combining.

If Days Fifteen and Sixteen are not convenient for you, then choose a couple of days later in the week or at the weekend when you are likely to be at home and don't have any important commitments. Rest and relax if you can. Take some gentle exercise and don't forget to practise your deep breathing.

If you are pregnant, diabetic or recovering from an illness, or are in any doubt about whether this detox programme is suitable for you, consult your doctor for advice.

Day Fifteen

On waking, drink a large cup of herb tea with a dribble of cold-pressed honey added, or a tumbler of filtered water, or boiled water with fresh lemon juice added.

For breakfast, enjoy a fresh fruit on its own or in combination and eat as much as you like; choose from kiwi fruit, apples, pears, grapes, mango, paw-paw, peaches or nectarines. If you are thirsty, drink a glass of diluted grape or apple juice (50:50 with water).

Midmorning, drink a cup of weak China or herb tea or a glass of water, followed by a banana. Chew the banana really thoroughly.

For lunch, choose a large raw salad containing any ingredients from the following list, served with a dressing of extra virgin olive oil and cider vinegar: Dark leaved lettuce, skinned cucumber, skinned tomato, cauliflower or broccoli florets, avocado pear, grated carrot, red, green or yellow peppers, spring onions (scallions), chicory, Chinese leaves, parsley, grated cabbage, celery or grated raw beetroot (not precooked, which usually contains preservative and won't be as nourishing anyway).

As a mid-afternoon snack, eat a handful of sunflower seeds, pumpkin seeds and unblanched almonds and drink a cup of water or weak herb tea.

For your evening meal, prepare a large portion of steamed or gently poached vegetables. Choose from leeks, cauliflower, cauliflower greens, broccoli, carrot, swede, turnip, parsnip, onion, marrow, celeriac, aubergine (eggplant), peppers, courgette (zucchini) or red cabbage. Add flavour with any culinary herbs, fresh if possible.

Before bed, eat a small carton of fresh plain additive-free bio-yoghurt.

Day Sixteen Detox

Repeat Day Fifteen, reversing the lunch and dinner if you like. Drink plenty of water throughout the two days and, if you feel hungry at any time, eat extra fruit or salad foods. Remember to wash all fruits and vegetables really thoroughly before use to remove as much dirt, bacteria and pesticide residue as possible. Get as much rest as you feel you need; practising your deep breathing exercises or listening to soothing music will help you to relax and will aid the detoxification process.

Day Seventeen – Take Care and Be Aware of Your Digestion

Just a reminder to be kinder to your digestive system so that your body will absorb maximum nourishment from your diet. Eating in too much of a hurry, grabbing food on the run, swallowing it all too quickly and rushing away as soon as the meal is finished is a recipe for disastrous digestion. If food isn't broken down properly, this results not only in poor absorption of nutrients but in toxicity caused by undigested food particles. Have sympathy with your stomach and appreciate how hard it works for you. Promise yourself that you'll make time to sit down to all your meals. Don't eat 'on the hoof', eat more slowly and chew food really thoroughly. Allow time between courses and remain seated for ten minutes after you have finished. Enjoy and be conscious of your food. All these things will further improve your digestion and help you to get the best nourishment from your new way of eating.

Day Eighteen – Minding Your Ps, As and Ss

As soon as your existing food stores were exhausted, I hope that you began to choose your meals from the meal suggestions provided on pages 136–167. If not, begin today.

All you have to do is to take one meal from the A list, one from the P list and one from the S list each day. A indicates 'Alkaline', P means 'Protein' and S stands for 'Starch'. If you are completely new to food combining and are still not familiar with these terms, it doesn't matter a bit so please don't worry. From now on, just eat three main meals every day from the selection provided, plus light healthy snacks between meals if you like. Have another look at the chart below; it's a useful guide to remembering how to balance daily intake:

Alkaline breakfast	means	Protein lunch and Starch dinner
	or	Starch lunch and Protein dinner
Protein breakfast	means	Starch lunch and Alkaline dinner
	or	Alkaline lunch and Starch dinner
Starch breakfast	means	Alkaline lunch and Protein dinner
	or	Protein lunch and Alkaline dinner

Day Nineteen –
Emphasizing the Importance of Fresh Fruit

Today it's worth underlining my absolutely essential food combiners' fruit rule: *Increase your intake of fresh*

*fruits (two or three pieces per day) but avoid eating them
with other food.* Treat fruit as a mid-morning or mid-
afternoon snack, as a starter to a meal or as a meal on
its own; in other words, take it only on an empty
stomach. Remember that fruit prefers 'free passage'
through the stomach and hates to be hindered by
concentrated proteins and starch foods. Eating fruit
with a main course or as a dessert means it is held up
by other foods; a common cause of indigestion, bloating
and flatulence in those with not-so-good digestive
systems!

Day Twenty –
Improving Overall Food Quality

Now is the time to have another look at Day Three and
at the chapter entitled 'Low Energy Foods'. This will
help you to cut down on the 'empty' calories which have
so little real nourishment and to introduce some of the
healthier alternatives. If you have been making use of
the meals on pages 133–67, the healthier options will
be almost automatic.

Once again, the need for occasional indulgences is
accepted, so please don't feel you can never have a
doughnut or plate of chips ever again. But do watch
those cakes, biscuits, sticky buns and chocolate. Why
not introduce a few healthier alternatives such as fresh
or dried fruit, unsalted nuts or seeds? Bananas are
sweet, nourishing and filling, so are dried figs. If you
buy or make cakes and biscuits, choose those made with
wholegrain flour and which use honey or molasses

instead of refined sugar as a sweetener. Carob-covered cereal bars can make a tasty treat.

Take the 'Low Energy List' with you when you go shopping — it will help you to avoid needless purchases and save money too.

Day Twenty-One – Adding Up the Exercise

On Day Seven we were talking about the importance of aerobic activity. A twenty- to thirty-minute brisk walk every day is an excellent way to add aerobic exercise to your healthy living programme. If possible, this should be in addition to any short extra distances you are walking between bus or tube stops. However, don't make a habit of walking or running near to heavy traffic — the pollution you breathe will be counter-productive to any possible benefits the additional activity might provide. Joggers who pound the main road alongside toxic exhaust fumes are doing themselves little or no good at all. A purposeful promenade in fresh air is one of the easiest ways to exercise — and it doesn't cost anything! Remember that exercise can overcome feelings of lethargy, but if you're very busy and find that you're genuinely too exhausted to exercise at the end of the day, try going to bed a little earlier and going for a walk first thing in the morning.

Don't forget to keep up the breathing exercises which you began on Day Fourteen.

Overview

What a positive week! You've given your system a thorough cleanse and rested and relaxed your digestion.

By reviewing the information on proteins and starches, food combining is now starting to fall into place. You have eaten more fruit and improved the overall quality of your diet, cutting down even further on processed, denatured foods. Boosting your aerobic activity and remembering to do your deep breathing exercises will have helped you to feel both relaxed and invigorated.

Week 4 (Days 22–30)

Totally Food Combining

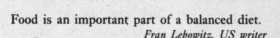

Food is an important part of a balanced diet.

Fran Lebowitz, US writer

> ### Aims For The Week
>
> This week you will be food combining for real! You will
> discover the importance of balancing your blood sugar
> and of making sure that you take some time for yourself.
> I'll be encouraging you to rediscover the pleasures of
> natural produce and to broaden your horizons when you
> visit the grocery store. Towards the end of the week you
> will find the Personal Symptom Analysis Review, to
> enable you to check your progress. You'll find out how
> food combining can become part of a healthier way of
> life – including enjoying the pleasures of eating out and
> entertaining at home.

Day Twenty-Two – Beating Blood Sugar Disease (How to Handle the 'Hypo')

One of the most common reasons for failing to stick to
a low-calorie weight-loss regime (which food combining is *not*, of course) is the 'hypo' (short for

hypoglycaemic attack). But low blood sugar doesn't affect only dieters; some nutrition experts believe it could be an epidemic condition which afflicts enormous numbers of people.

When petrol is fed into a motor vehicle, the internal combustion engine converts the fuel into gas to produce energy. If poor-quality fuel is used, the engine cannot function at peak performance. If the fuel is allowed to run dry, then the vehicle will have no power at all.

In a similar way, food is converted into a special body fuel called glucose which supplies the system with energy. The levels of glucose are stabilized by hormones which act as a balancing mechanism. If the concentration of fuel (glucose) is too high, insulin is produced by the pancreas to bring it down. If it falls too low, glucagon — also from the pancreas — and adrenalin from the adrenal glands are sent for; they help to draw glucose from reserve supplies in the liver to restore the status quo. Those reserves are kept topped up by visits to the 'petrol station': your regular meals. But if you miss meals, don't eat enough or fill up with inferior fodder, the glucose levels fall too far and cannot be restored. The result: a hypoglycaemic attack, which is also known as low blood sugar or low blood glucose.

Dieters suffer because they try to subsist on quantities of food that wouldn't sustain a sparrow, so are not eating enough to maintain this equilibrium. When glucose levels tumble, a range of extremely unpleasant symptoms can be triggered: dizziness, insomnia, night sweats, hollow hunger pangs, weak muscles or sudden loss of energy to name but a few. Persistent neglect of the fuel reserves (for example, missing meals altogether or simply not eating enough at each session) can lead to debilitating fatigue and chronic illness. More seriously, if hypoglycaemia is allowed to run riot and is left untreated, diabetes may be the result.

But hypoglycaemia doesn't only haunt dieters; it's an increasingly common condition which affects large numbers of people of all dietary persuasions. The first part of the body to suffer when blood sugar falls is the brain. Little wonder then that poor co-ordination, forgetfulness, odd sensations of feeling 'spaced out', light headedness, lack of concentration and irritability can also be familiar and frequent.

Food combining helps to overcome these problems because it properly nourishes and nurtures the system. Breakfasts are more than adequate to keep you going until lunch but, should you need a pit stop, don't be afraid to sortie into the snack list on page 77.

If balancing your blood sugar has been a problem in the past, food combining will almost certainly fix it. Beat those cravings for good by following these additional tips:

- Hit the hypo where it hurts by eating when you are hungry. Don't suffer weakness and emptiness just because it's a while until lunch or dinner.
- If you are away from base, carry a snack with you. Keep a few cereal bars, nuts and seeds in your car, briefcase or handbag.
- Steer clear of foods that are made with refined flour and refined sugars; they goad the pancreas and adrenal glands into hyperactivity and make hypoglycaemia worse.

- Instead of white flour, white rice and refined cereals, choose wholegrain alternatives such as oats, brown rice, brown pasta and whole rye. These 'complex carbohydrates' release their energy more slowly into the system and keep blood sugar in check.

- Choose close-grained wholemeal bread instead of the spongy and elastic sliced loaves.

- Choose starchy and sustaining jacket potatoes instead of fat-soaked french fries.

- Eat oat biscuits, rice cakes or rye crackers instead of sweet biscuits.

- Don't miss out on meals in the mistaken belief that not eating will bring faster weight loss. It won't.

- Always have breakfast. If you can't face food first thing, then eat a couple of pieces of fruit as soon as you can manage them but don't leave it until lunchtime before you eat.

- Remember that too much coffee, tea, cola, sugar or artificial sweeteners can make hypo attacks much more likely and more frequent.

- Try to avoid short-term sugar fixes such as sweets and chocolate, soft drinks, sticky buns, cakes or biscuits. They may give you relief for half an hour or so but, in doing so, will put serious strain on all the body systems which are responsible for blood sugar balance.

- Try to cut down on added sugar. As a temporary measure (and instead of artificial sweeteners), switch to fruit sugar (fructose powder). It looks and tastes just like ordinary sugar but is nearly twice the sweetness so that you need use only half the quantity. Then, slowly and gradually, wean yourself off it a grain or two at a time (literally). Or use honey and cut down by degrees. An even better alternative is something called frugo-oligosaccharide, or fructolite for short, a naturally sweet substitute suitable for baking and for beverages. Fructolite does not aggravate candida and encourages rather than damages the good bacteria in the gut; both hypoglycaemics and those with high cholesterol would find it a good alternative to other sugars (see Resources).

- Ease up on added salt and on salty snacks. Too much sodium can be just as devastating to hypoglycaemics as sugar, putting a strain on the body's hormone balance and causing a dramatic fall in the levels of the mineral potassium which is needed for the metabolism of glucose.
- Have a light snack before going to bed. A small amount of food taken later on in the evening helps to keep blood sugar balanced while you sleep. Whilst it's true that a heavy meal eaten late in the evening can keep you awake all night, an empty stomach can do the same. Many an insomniac with night starvation will slip into a sound slumber after a warm drink and a biscuit, a bowl of cereal or a few spoonsful of yoghurt.
- Redress the stress by practising those deep breathing exercises explained on Day Fourteen. Uncontrolled stress and anxiety lay unnecessary strain on the body's hormonal system, part of which is also responsible for blood sugar balance.
- Eat little and often.

- Enjoy your between-meal snacks.
- Watch your weight. The hormones that balance blood glucose may have to work overtime if you are either seriously under- or seriously overweight.
- Be sensible about alcohol. Excesses can play havoc with blood glucose and can push it to dangerously low levels.
- Most important of all, don't ignore hypoglycaemic symptoms. Left uncontrolled, they could trigger diabetes.

Important Note
Exhaustion and lethargy have many different causes. If you suffer with chronic fatigue all the time, irrespective of what and when you eat, then it is unlikely that your tiredness is linked to hypoglycaemia. If energy levels are not improving within two weeks of commencing your new diet, then you should consult your medical adviser without further delay.

Day Twenty-Three — Rediscover the Pleasures of Natural Produce

Now that you are more familiar with those stamina-sapping low-energy foods, as discussed on Day Three, it's likely that you have investigated a few of the alternative suggestions that I make in the 'Low-Energy Foods' section on page 105. Now it's time to be even more adventurous. Study the fruits and vegetables lists on pages 126–131 and then, next time you visit the grocery store or supermarket, make a resolution to be more daring. Also, look out for farm shops, market stalls and organic produce. At each visit, try just one new fruit or vegetable or salad food that you have never eaten before. Broadening your horizons in this way will more than make up for those few food combinations that don't mix well together.

Make the most of your fruit and vegetables! There is so much out there that's different. And don't be afraid to ask for help. Lots of stores have information leaflets and booklets which give advice on nutritional values, storage, ripening times and recipes.

And if you haven't tried them before, now is the time to experiment with fresh vegetable juices. They are cleansing, refreshing and delicious and many people prefer them to fruit juices. You can also mix vegetable and fruit juices if you enjoy them that way. Here are some of my favourite combinations:

- Carrot and cucumber
- Celery and tomato
- Or, for a really cleansing aperitif, try carrot, celery, raw beetroot, apple and grape!

Day Twenty-Four—Keep Things Simple

You have learned a lot over the last three and a half weeks and have done a great deal to enhance your general health and well-being. One of the keys to continued success is to memorize these simple food combining rules:

- Don't mix starches or sugary foods with proteins
- Don't eat fruit with starches or proteins

- Wherever possible, eat: one protein-based meal, one starch-based meal and, one completely alkaline-forming meal each day
- Remember that fruits, vegetables and salads are alkaline-forming
- Remember that proteins and starches are acid-forming
- Remember that neutral foods are those that mix with anything

Day Twenty-Five – Important Health Tips

Remember to follow as many of these important health tips as you can and you will be taking real steps towards enjoying a healthier way of life:

- Drink more water
- Drink less tea and coffee
- Cut down on processed foods
- Go easy on the sugar
- Chuck out the chip pan
- Take regular exercise
- Breathe more deeply
- Eat more slowly
- Get plenty of sleep
- Make time to rest and relax

Days Twenty-Six and Twenty-Seven – Entertaining With Food Combining

Eating out and entertaining at home using food combining guidelines is easier that you think. On Days Twenty-Six and Twenty-Seven, why not plan a food combining dinner engagement for some friends or work colleagues or just for you and your partner?

Just remember the basics of keeping proteins and starches away from each other and of eating fruit separately. Make it a leisurely meal and leave plenty of time between courses. Why not start with a fruit medley of fresh pineapple, kiwi and mango; follow it with a fish dish and a colourful salad or vegetable variety and make a deliciously creamy dessert with yoghurt and cream. Or begin with a vegetable soup or consommé, followed with a nut salad and a pasta or rice dish. The menus on page 134 should give you some bright ideas.

Dining Out

When you are eating out, study the menu carefully and choose items that are not ladled with rich sauces or likely to cause combination catastrophes. For example, steer clear of the cheese which so often comes with pasta. If you're having poultry, meat or fish, avoid the potatoes which usually turn up with the vegetable selection and say no to the regulation French fries – but do serve yourself extra vegetables or salad to compensate. If a starch meal is your fancy, ask for a large jacket potato, sauté potatoes or rice dish with an extra portion of salad or vegetables. After you have been food combining at home for a few weeks, successful mixing and matching in restaurants becomes second nature. Most establishments are willing to be flexible and make alterations to the menu to suit your dietary preferences. Don't be afraid to ask.

Day Twenty-Eight –
Taking Care of Number One

Today is all about looking after yourself. Learning how to relax (and how to deal with stress) is a fundamental part of any successful fitness programme. The *right* kind of stress, in moderation, can be positively beneficial, stimulating and encouraging; but if your ability to cope is poor, it's likely that your digestion will be under stress too. Ulcers, for example, are said to be the result of 'undigested stress'. If you don't break your food down efficiently, nutrients won't be properly absorbed and the body won't be fed, repaired or supplied with energy. Before you know it, you're part of a vicious circle of stress, exhaustion and illness which in turn leads to more stress.

There are lots of ways of making life's labours easier to live with. Potentially, stress can affect anyone – but not everyone suffers. It depends upon how you perceive stress, how you react to it and how you cope. The same stressor could stimulate one person into positive or ambitious action and another into deep depression and gloom.

When stress affects you in a detrimental way, it's not just one isolated part of your body that suffers (e.g. a headache, a sore throat, a chest infection, a bout of indigestion or an aching back can all be triggered by excess stress); it's the whole body, every cell, every blood vessel and every organ including, of course, the heart. How many times do we hear about someone being struck down by premature heart disease who was also under a lot of pressure? Sadly, all too often. In continually stressful circumstances where there is no let up, the body can lose its 'punch', become more prone to illness and certainly no match for the latest virus. Researchers have concluded that people who are stressed by life's burdensome events such as bereavement, moving house, changing jobs, being burgled, becoming unemployed or passed over for promotion are much more likely to catch a cold!

Relaxation is not a luxury, it's an absolute necessity for life. So don't feel guilty about looking after yourself. Treat yourself to what Americans so accurately call 'quality time'. Here are a few tried and tested stress relievers:

- Organize a regular aromatherapy massage and ask your therapist to recommend some relaxing oils for you to use at home, in the bath water, in an oil burner or aromastream unit.
- Put 4 or 5 drops of lavender oil in a warm bath, relax for ten minutes and then go straight to bed.
- Find out about reflexology and how it can help reduce stress levels.
- Visit the hairdresser or beauty salon – or if you are housebound or too busy to go, ask about home visits; there are plenty of beauticians, hairstylists and therapists who are happy to come to you.

- Take up a regular sporting activity, join a club or meet regularly with friends.
- Use relaxation cassette tapes or CDs. Or just drift off to your favourite classical music or instrumental.
- Take a walk every day.
- Practise your deep breathing exercises every day and at any time when you are particularly anxious, as outlined on Day Fourteen. Stressed and agitated people breathe too shallowly, encouraging a build-up of carbon dioxide in the system and tension in the muscles. Taking a deep breath and sighing helps to release lots of built-up tension.
- Planning ahead and being well organized can remove a lot of life's stressors before they actually arrive. But worrying unnecessarily about things outside your control is not healthy. Remember that yesterday has gone and by the time tomorrow comes, it's today.
- Join a class; learn a new skill.
- Try yoga, tai chi or other meditation.
- If you are really uptight, take a herbal medicine that contains valerian or passiflora; take a low dosage every day for a couple of months and see if things improve.
- Get out of bed 15 minutes earlier in the morning. You'll cope far better with your day if you don't start out in a panic.
- Tell yourself that every appointment, visit or journey begins 15 minutes earlier than it really does. That way, you're more likely to arrive on time. Some people even set their wrist watches and clocks accordingly!

- Write your appointments in a diary or on a notepad. Expecting your brain to keep tabs on everything can be exhausting and stressful. Remember the old Chinese proverb which says that the palest ink is better than the most retentive memory.
- Think ahead. Assume that your fuel tank is empty when it is still a quarter full. That way, you'll never run out of petrol.
- Shop for emergencies. Always keep supplies of cards or coins for public telephones and toilets, postage stamps for that urgent letter, plasters for the first aid box etc.
- Don't put off tasks you don't like. Get them out of the way early in the day, then you'll have more pleasurable things to look forward to.
- Get plenty of sleep.
- If possible, sleep with the window open. Breathing in your own stale air all night won't be conducive to improved health and well-being.
- Whatever the season, open the window wide first thing in the morning and fill your lungs with fresh air. (Remember to close and lock the window before you leave the house!)
- Always carry a book or magazine with you. If you are held up in a queue, time will pass more quickly and less stressfully.
- Get ready for the next day the night before, including deciding what you will wear.
- Say 'No' sometimes. Being constantly on call is a definite health hazard.
- Laugh – at life and at yourself. Don't take everything so seriously. Research shows that

laughter stabilizes heart rate and blood pressure, boosts immunity and shifts anger! One minute of laughter can benefit the body and mind as much as half an hour of deep relaxation! A good laugh brings relief, release and comfort.

- Don't allow yourself to be burdened or bothered by defeatists, miseries or worriers. Someone else's negative thoughts can bring down your own mood.

- Talk out your troubles with a trustworthy friend.

- If someone angers you, don't hit back. Instead, distance yourself from the person or situation and verbalize your annoyance and displeasure to an empty room. Counting to 100 or even 1000 or waiting 24 hours before dealing with the situation usually renders any further action unnecessary.

- If drowsiness creeps up on you during the day, catnap for five minutes, take a short break, get some fresh air or turn your attention to a different job and go back to the other one later. A lot of daytime tiredness comes more from boredom or overexposure to a repetitive task than from genuine exhaustion. If your brain is weary, it's easy for your body to feel worn out, too.

- Every day, plan to do something you really enjoy.

- Count your blessings and be grateful for good things. There is always someone worse off than yourself. When my husband was in hospital, frail and afraid, wired up to millions of pounds' worth of equipment and trying to recover from the shock of two very major operations for cancer and peritonitis, he counted his blessings every day. His exceptional surgeon and nursing staff, his friends, family, get well cards and the autumn tints in the trees outside his window were all on his list. He knows that this kind of positive thinking was just one of the things that pulled him through.

- Remember that proper food combinations can improve the way the body digests and absorbs stress-fighting nutrients, leading to more energy and a stronger immune system.
- Looking after yourself (as opposed to running yourself ragged for everyone else) is not a crime, it's an absolute necessity. So, from today, follow the above tips and give yourself some space. Go ahead and book that regular aromatherapy massage or reflexology treatment. Make time for your deep breathing and walking. Book an appointment at the hairdresser or the beauty salon. Resolve to take a half hour break every day to read, cat nap or simply heed the words of W.H. Davies and take time to stand and stare.

Emergency De-Stressors

If something panics or frightens you or just winds you up, try one of these emergency measures:

Keeping the mouth gently closed, inhale deeply through the nose to a count of six, then exhale pushing the air out through the mouth in a big sigh. Repeat four times.

OR

Inhale through the nose to a count of seven. Exhale through the mouth to a count of eight. Breathe in again to a count of seven and breathe out, this time, to a count of nine. Breathe in a third time to a count of seven and breathe out to a count of ten.

If you are unsure about how slowly or quickly to count on the in-breath, say to yourself the words 'one, peaceful', 'two, peaceful', 'three, peaceful', 'four, peaceful', etc.

Important Note
If you have a heart condition or blood pressure disorder, check with your G.P. before doing these breathing exercises.

Day Twenty-Nine – Reviewing The Results

Personal Symptom Analysis Review

Fill out the following questionnaire and then check the list of symptoms against those that you noted down on Day One.

	None	Less Frequent	No Change
Regular headaches	____	____	____
Migraine	____	____	____
Indigestion	____	____	____
Heartburn	____	____	____
Abdominal pain after eating	____	____	____
Bloating	____	____	____
Flatulence	____	____	____
Coated tongue	____	____	____
Constipation	____	____	____
Diarrhoea	____	____	____
Irritable Bowel	____	____	____

	None	Less Frequent	No Change
Catarrh	_____	_____	_____
Recurring sore throat	_____	_____	_____
Persistent infections	_____	_____	_____
Chronic fatigue	_____	_____	_____
Muscle weakness	_____	_____	_____
Muscle spasm	_____	_____	_____
Sudden tiredness	_____	_____	_____
Lack of energy	_____	_____	_____
Aching joints	_____	_____	_____
Restless, twitchy limbs	_____	_____	_____
A need for frequent meals	_____	_____	_____
Dizziness	_____	_____	_____
Palpitations	_____	_____	_____
Night sweats	_____	_____	_____
Day sweats	_____	_____	_____
Excessive thirst	_____	_____	_____
Anxiety	_____	_____	_____
Irritability	_____	_____	_____
Bleeding gums	_____	_____	_____
Mouth ulcers	_____	_____	_____
Allergies	_____	_____	_____
Poor circulation	_____	_____	_____

Make a note of any other symptoms which you listed at the beginning of the programme but which are not included above.

_____ _____ _____ _____

_____ _____ _____ _____

_____ _____ _____ _____

_____ _____ _____ _____

Over the past four weeks, you should have noticed enhanced energy levels, better weight control and improvements in your general health. Your hard-working system has been cleansed and nourished and you have learned enough to food combine seriously and enjoyably.

If you have been following food combining in order to lose weight and find that your weight has not altered a great deal, then that does not mean that either you — or the diet — has failed. On the contrary, it is extremely common for weight to be lost only very slowly whilst food combining (or to increase equally slowly if you are trying to put on a few additional pounds). This is the safe way to balance bodyweight. Lose it too quickly and it will be back before you know it! In addition, by losing weight the food combining way you'll have more energy and be less inclined to suffer from those destructive bouts of bingeing or uncontrollable cravings which end up breaking your resolve.

It is also vitally important to bear in mind what I said on Day One that, in nutritional terms, 30 days is a relatively short period of time. Some symptoms will almost certainly take longer than a month to resolve, especially if they have been troubling you for many months or even years. Any that particularly concern you should, of course, be referred to your family physician.

Important Note
The health tips, food combining guidelines and symptom check list contained in this manual are not prescriptive nor are they an attempt to diagnose or treat any condition or patient. It is recommended that you keep your doctor informed of any changes you are making to your diet and of any supplement programme you choose to follow.

Day Thirty — Time For Congratulations

You've made it! You're a qualified food combiner. By now, the old cravings should be diminishing and the body feeling fitter. You've learned lots about low-energy foods and the healthy alternatives. Your system has been given a thorough cleanse and your digestion a rest. You've taken more exercise, learned to breathe more efficiently and taken time off to care for yourself.

As explained on page 29, *Food Combining In 30 Days* puts you on the food combining road to good health for life. It is not meant as a quick-fix diet programme or something that you 'go on' and 'come off'. Now that you know the basics, why not continue?

And please let me emphasize, once again, the importance of *enjoying* your meals. Food combining should be fun, not an obsessive slog. If, for some reason, you can't food combine every single day, don't worry; the rules are not written in tablets of stone. If you fancy fish and chips once in a while, have an uncontrollable craving for cheese and biscuits or a Sunday roast with meat and potatoes, go for it and enjoy it. If you're eating out at someone else's home and you're offered proteins and starches together or fruit salad as a dessert, then go for that too. You should still gain considerable benefit if you food combine for, say, five days out of every seven.

Food Combining In 30 Days is, of necessity, a simple guide to food combining and healthier living. If you would like to progress to other food combining books and health guides that contain more elaborate recipes and additional detail, please turn to the Recommended Reading list on page 171.

3

Food Combining Plus

Low-Energy Foods

The 'energy' referred to here has nothing to do with calories which are, of course, units of energy: in this context, 'low-energy' means foods that are of poor nutritional value to the body. Some may be high in calories, yet if consumed in excess are likely actually to sap energy and lead to increased fatigue. Notice that they are either high in fat, sugar or additives or have unacceptable starch/protein combinations. Many may appear to be filling but are otherwise not overly endowed with nourishment! Small quantities are unlikely to be harmful and I'm not suggesting that you give up all of them altogether. However, excesses can overload the system and will not be helpful to your new way of healthy eating.

In the section on weight problems (page 20), we read that toxicity can drag your energy down. Learning about the detrimental effects of low-energy foods will help to guide you towards the best food purchases in the grocery store or supermarket. Where applicable, a brief explanation and a list of alternatives are given.

The Low-Energy List

Remember that acid-forming foods are marked '-', alkaline-forming foods with a '+' and neutral foods 'n'. Nearly all low-energy foods are acid-forming.

- − Sweets and chocolate
- − Brown or white sugar
- − Artificial sweeteners
- − Artificial colours, flavours and preservatives
- − Coffee, tea, cocoa, cola, hot chocolate
- − Alcohol
- − Pasteurized orange juice
- n Tap water
- − Cow's milk and soya milk
- − White flour and bread
- n Most polyunsaturated spreads
- n Most cooking oils
- n Manufactured/processed 'low-fat' foods
- − Salt
- − Salty snacks
- − Peanuts
- − Beef, pork and related products
- − Battery-raised poultry and battery and barn eggs
- − Processed, smoked and coloured cheeses
- − Charcoaled or burned food
- − Deep-fried foods
- − Pizzas, pastries, pies and pasta

Cut Down On: Sweets and Chocolate

ALTERNATIVE CHOICES

Carob chocolate, fruit bars, cereal bars, dried fruit (figs are especially good), unblanched almonds, natural licorice and sesame halva. Health food stores usually stock a wide range of healthier sweet treats.

Avoid: Brown or White Sugar

ALTERNATIVE CHOICES

Blackstrap molasses, honey, crystallized ginger or real maple syrup. Remember, brown sugar is no healthier than white! If you need white sugar for baking, use fruit sugar (also called fructose powder; see Resources), which is almost twice the sweetness of ordinary sugar so use half the quantity. Keep all sweetenings to a minimum.

Avoid: Artificial Sweeteners

ALTERNATIVE CHOICES

As above. Evidence is mounting that artificial sweeteners may disturb the blood glucose levels and increase cravings just as severely as pure sugar. These chemical compounds also have a relatively short history and no-one can really say if long-term use is likely to be beneficial or hazardous to our health.

Avoid: Foods That Contain Artificial Colours, Flavours and Preservatives

ALTERNATIVE CHOICES

Buy fresh wherever possible. It is well-known that certain additives are responsible for hyperactivity and headaches. Like sweeteners, the long-term effects are unknown. In our modern society of processed everything, it can be difficult to avoid additives completely. Indeed, in certain cases, they may be vital to prevent food spoiling prematurely, but some products are simply overloaded with unnecessary E numbers. It's really worthwhile buying a book on additives so that you know which ones are artificial and potentially harmful and which are natural with no toxic problems. For example, E110 Sunset Yellow is made from coal tar derivatives whilst E101 is Riboflavin (Vitamin B_2). Both provide bright yellow colouring!

Cut Down On: Coffee, Tea, Cocoa, Cola, Hot Chocolate

No need to give these up, just be sensible about intake.

ALTERNATIVE CHOICES

Herbal, fruit and green teas like Jasmine, coffee substitutes, fruit and vegetable juices and water. Or choose the better quality 'normal' teas, which tend to be naturally lower in caffeine than the cheaper brands.
See Resources for further information.

Cut Down On: Alcohol

Again, unless it's your own decision, no-one expects you to give up your favourite tipple. But keep beer and spirits to an absolute minimum and drink wine in moderation. Some research recommends that moderate wine drinking is positively beneficial! As with most things, it's the excesses that are damaging.

Choose Wisely: Orange Juice

In my experience in treating patients with headaches, migraine and arthritis, some brands of ordinary orange juice or orange drink can bring on or aggravate the pain associated with these conditions.

ALTERNATIVE CHOICES

If you are an orange juice fan, buy the additive-free freshly squeezed juice or prepare your own at home. Or choose organic apple or grape juice instead.

Avoid: Tap Water

ALTERNATIVE CHOICES

For drinking purposes and for filling the kettle, filtered water is the best option – and cheaper than in bottles. Rely on bottled water when you are travelling, eating out or away from home.

Avoid: Cow's Milk and Soya Milk

There are some people who find soya milk a useful alternative to cow's milk but I have yet to be convinced that either of these is a healthy option. More properly *soya drink*; soya milk is a processed food and is acid-forming. It can be very difficult indeed to digest and its nutrients are not well absorbed. It is a 'fortified' food — which generally means that it is not sufficiently nourishing in its natural state to be marketed without being supplemented. I have also seen patients whose eczema, asthma and allergies have worsened when they introduced soya milk to their diets.

Cow's milk is an emotive food. For example, the prevalence of osteoporosis and the belief that cow's milk is a good source of calcium perpetuate the myth that the use of one will reduce the risk of the other. In addition, it is still widely believed that, in order to breast feed successfully, pregnant mothers must drink copious quantities of cow's milk. In fact, babies with cow's milk allergy, eczema, colic, sleeplessness, persistent infections and diarrhoea are a likely consequence of such erroneous practices. Asthma, eczema, digestive and bowel disorders appear to be made worse in many adults who drink cow's milk.

Cow's milk is an excellent food source for calves but for humans it is a common allergen, associated with a wide range of illnesses.

As long ago as 1547, in his *Dietary of Health*, Andrew Boorde warned his readers that 'Cow's milk is not good for them which have gurgulations in the belly'. Indeed, over the years I have seen many new patients with digestive difficulties, bowel disorders, catarrh and other conditions related to an over-production of mucus whose problems resolved once milk was removed from the diet. It is a myth that cow's milk is good food for humans; we remain the only species on this planet that maintains the very unnatural practice of, voluntarily, drinking the milk of another species. Nor is cow's milk a good source of calcium for human beings. Once pasteurized, milk becomes acid-forming. The heat process alters its basic structure and, apart from disturbing its enzyme and protein content, the calcium is rendered far less absorbable.

ALTERNATIVE CHOICES

Goat's milk or sheep's milk in small quantities, buttermilk or plain yoghurt. Calcium is available from a wide variety of other foods too, including green leafy vegetables, canned fish, cheese and grains.

Avoid: White Flour and Bread

ALTERNATIVE CHOICES

Good-quality bread, made with wholegrain flour, is an excellent source of dietary fibre and nutrients. However, I have seen many, many cases where certain kinds of bread (particularly the very soft — usually sliced — supermarket loaves) bring on extreme fatigue. One reason may be that, for extra softness, these loaves contain large amounts of gluten and yeast, both potential allergens. Good alternatives are yeast-free soda bread, black rye or pumpernickel and wholewheat pitta bread. You could also try rye crackers, oat biscuits and rice cakes. For cooking, use organic wholegrain flour as an alternative to white. If you are one of the few who cannot tolerate the fibre in brown bread (it can cause severe digestive discomfort in some people), use organic, additive-free white bread and organic unbleached white flour.

Avoid: Polyunsaturated Spreads made from Hydrogenated Vegetable Oils

Whether low-fat or not, any 'margarine' made with hydrogenated vegetable oils (check the labels) is not recommended. Evidence continues to mount that these manufactured fats are not the healthy alternative to butter that the media hype would have us believe. Studies show that hydrogenated spreads *increase* rather than decrease the risk of coronary heart disease and could be implicated in a range of other serious illnesses including cancer.

ALTERNATIVE CHOICES

Use small quantities of butter or non-hydrogenated fat (from the health food store).

Avoid: Processed Cooking Oils

Buy only the best quality (cold-pressed, unprocessed) polyunsaturated oils for salad dressings and use only extra virgin olive oil for cooking. Whatever you may hear or read about polyunsaturates being good for you, the bottom line is that they are not if they're processed, heated or subjected to light, air or radiation. So never, never cook with polyunsaturated oils; keep them for cold uses only and store them carefully. Use extra virgin olive oil for cooking.

In my books *The Food Combining Diet* and *Kathryn*

Marsden's Super Skin (both published by Thorsons) you'll find additional information on fats and oils, explaining in more detail which are healthy, which should be avoided and why.

Avoid: Manufactured/Processed 'Low-Fat' Foods

Take care when choosing cheeses, yoghurts, fromage frais, mayonnaise and other foods which carry low-fat, low-cholesterol or low-calorie labels. Many of them contain masses of additives and some have hydrogenated vegetable oils too. So do read the labels.

ALTERNATIVE CHOICES

Be moderate. Choose the full-fat, additive-free version and eat less of it.

Avoid: Salt and Salty Foods

There is so much hidden salt around us (added to packaged foods by the manufacturer) that it can be difficult to track down. The foods that contain it may not necessarily taste salty. All in all, most of us eat far too much of it. Watch out for it (usually labelled as sodium) in breakfast cereals, all manner of canned foods, tinned and preserved meats, ready meals and, of course, ready-salted snacks such as crisps and peanuts. If in doubt, read the labels. Many sweet foods also have salt in their lists of ingredients – and salt can upset blood glucose levels in the body just as severely as can sugar!

ALTERNATIVE CHOICES

If you need sprinkled salt, choose sea salt or lo-salt (sparingly) but do not add it to the cooking water — it leaches out important nutrients. Add extra flavour with herbs.

Avoid: Peanuts

Unless they are organic and absolutely fresh, peanuts can carry a fungus called an aflatoxin. Experts are concerned that it may have carcinogenic properties.

ALTERNATIVE CHOICES

Unblanched almonds, Brazil nuts, hazelnuts (filberts), pecans, pine nuts, cashews. Make sure they're absolutely fresh.

Avoid: Beef, Pork and Related Products

Unless they are truly organic, the meat from cows and pigs is not recommended for food combiners — or for anyone who wants to eat healthily. Apart from the risks of BSE, drug misuse and antibiotic and steroid residues, these meats can be extremely difficult to digest. I have also seen cases of severe gastric upset, aggravated bowel disorders and sickness caused by the ingestion of beef and pork.

ALTERNATIVE CHOICES

Free-range poultry, lamb, rabbit, turkey and fish are good alternatives for non-vegetarians.

Avoid: Battery-Raised Poultry and Battery and Barn Eggs

ALTERNATIVE CHOICES

True free-range eggs and free-range poultry.

Avoid: Processed, Smoked and Coloured Cheeses

The smoking process and colourings have been known to cause allergies and stomach irritation. Better to choose your hard cheeses 'off the round' where possible. Avoid plastic wrappings if you can and cheeses that contain additives.

ALTERNATIVE CHOICES

Any that have not been tampered with!

Avoid: Charcoaled, Smoked and Burnt Food

There is some concern that these kinds of foods may be responsible for causing stomach cancer. They certainly seem to aggravate pre-existing digestive disorders and are best avoided except for the infrequent special occasion barbecue or treat of smoked salmon.

Avoid: Deep-Fried Foods

Common-sense says that anything deep-fried is going to be high in fat.

ALTERNATIVE CHOICES

Shallow-fry in olive oil (great for healthy chips or scallops), steam, sauté, stir-fry, grill, bake, poach or casserole your cooked foods.

Cut down on: Pizzas, Pastries, Pies and Pasta

No need to give up these foods but do be aware that they can be poor starch/protein combinations. For example, pizza bases, pasta and pastry are starchy but the fillings, toppings and garnishes most commonly used with them are protein i.e. cheese, egg, fish, bacon etc. Go for neutral vegetable or salad toppings. Avoid quiche (egg, cheese and milk = protein, base = starch) and remember that pasta should be the egg-free variety, served without cheese.

Nutrient Supplements

> Common sense in medicine is the master workman.
>
> *Peter Mere Latham (1789–1875), US poet and essayist*

The Need For Nutrient Supplements

In an ideal world, we would obtain all the health-giving nutrients we need from a varied and balanced diet. Indeed, one of the many benefits of food combining is the fact that absorption of nourishment is markedly increased. Unfortunately, however, whilst we can control how we combine our food, few of us can influence how it is grown, treated, stored, transported or displayed before we purchase it.

In addition, our bodies also act as unwilling 'pollution sponges', soaking up poor-quality air and toxic fumes by the lung load. To defend itself against the ravages of environmental contaminants, the body calls upon its reserves of antioxidant protectors – special nutrients which know how to repair the damage to cells and tissues. But if there aren't enough nutrients around – because of a shortfall in supply or an increased demand – immune strength is diminished and repairs cannot be carried out.

As a practitioner with many years' experience in the use of supplements and diet in the treatment of disease, I am a firm believer that the application of low-dose, top-quality vitamins and minerals can be of enormous therapeutic value both in the treatment of existing disease and as a preventive measure against illness occurring. They are especially helpful to those who have spent years on less-than-nourishing low-calorie diet regimes. I think that the samples from our mailbag (see pages 7–10) provide clear evidence of their importance in helping to overcome both serious and minor illnesses.

The first list below gives *you* the opportunity to check out *your* own nutritional health. The second section is a 'pollution test'. If you answer yes to more than three of the questions in each section, it may be that a course of multivitamins would be a worthwhile investment. Beware, however: the market is flooded with poor-quality products. The suppliers listed in Resources (page 174) are well-known for their high standards of service and product quality and will be happy to advise you.

Nutrition Quiz

- My workload is so heavy that I tend to miss one or more meals each day.
- I work in a stuffy office atmosphere and rarely get out into the fresh air or daylight.
- I never take exercise.
- I travel to work each day in very heavy traffic.

- I smoke.
- I take regular prescribed and/or over-the-counter medication.
- I suffer from excessive stress/anxiety/depression.
- I have jaw, gum, tooth or mouth problems which make it difficult for me to eat.
- I have a medical condition or illness which affects my appetite.
- I suffer frequently with indigestion/heartburn/bloating/flatulence/constipation.
- I live alone and tend not to bother too much over meals.
- I have gained more than 1 stone (14 lbs/6 kg) in weight over the last 6 months without wanting to.
- I always seem to be following one weight-loss diet or another.
- I hate vegetables.
- I eat take-aways or packeted ready meals more than once a week.
- I have a sweet tooth and eat sugary foods every day.
- I drink more than six cups of tea and coffee each day.
- I drink more than two alcoholic drinks every day.

Pollution Quiz

Now have a look at this checklist and see if you think you are regularly exposed to any of these items:

- Pesticides, fungicides and herbicides
- Excess nitrates and other fertilizers
- Drug and hormone residues in animal products
- Radiation, irradiation, microwaves, electromagnetics
- Heavy metal contamination i.e. mercury, aluminium, cadmium, lead

- Industrial pollution, acid rain, contaminated rivers and water supplies
- Food processing
- Vehicle exhaust emissions
- Artificial colours, flavours and preservatives
- High-fat, high-sugar, high-salt foods
- Excess alcohol
- Cigarette smoke
- Crash dieting, bingeing, eating disorders
- Prescribed medication, the Pill, HRT
- Stress, distress, anxiety, depression, illness
- Lack of exercise
- Too much tea and coffee
- Missed and hurried meals, poor digestion
- Weight problems

If you decide to use supplements, there is no need to use lots of different products or munch masses of different vitamins and minerals. A good-quality multivitamin/mineral complex with extra vitamin C and, perhaps, essential fatty acids in the form of GLA or evening primrose oil are usually enough to provide that extra protection. If you have a tendency to suffer with persistent infections, have been prescribed more than one course of antibiotics in the past twelve months or are plagued with constipation, bloating or irritable bowel syndrome, a probiotic supplement will help to re-establish the friendly gut flora. (See Resources for further information.)

Hypoglycaemics are a special case when it comes to supplementation. Reactive hypoglycaemia responds well to dietary change but also benefits from the use of the trace mineral chromium together with B complex vitamins. Chromium is part of a molecule which helps to balance insulin production and, according to the results of studies carried out by the United States Department of Agriculture, is believed to be deficient in large numbers of the population.

If you have followed several very low-fat diets over a number of years, you may be short of essential fatty acids and need additional supplements of GLA or evening primrose oil.

When choosing supplements, please remember:
- Read the pack instructions carefully.
- *Never* exceed the stated dose.
- Vitamins and minerals are not meal replacements or substitutes for nourishing food.
- Swallow supplements in the middle of a meal, unless specifically advised to take them on an empty stomach.
- Don't expect overnight miracles. Nutrient supplements may take several weeks or months to make their mark on the nutritional deficiencies which have built up slowly over many years.
- If you are on prescribed medication or under the care of your hospital consultant or G.P., you are advised to talk to them before commencing any supplement programme or changing your diet.

4

Food Lists and Recipes

Food Lists

◡

Proteins *(see Day Four, page 36)*

Remember the fundamental rule of food combining: Proteins and Starches should always be eaten separately. Concentrated Proteins are:

- Meat
- Poultry
- Offal
- Cheese
- Eggs

- Fish
- Shellfish
- Soya Beans
- All Soya-based Products
+ Yoghurt

Starches *(see Day Five, page 39)*

Concentrated starches include:

CEREALS AND GRAINS
(ALL ACID-FORMING EXCEPT MILLET)

- Barley
- Buckwheat
- Bulgur (Burghul)
- Corn (Maize)

- Brown Rice
- Basmati Rice
- Rice Bran
- Rice Cakes

- Couscous
- Cracked Wheat
- Macaroni
- Maize (Corn)
- Matzo Meal
+ Millet
- Oat Bran
- Oats
- Oat Cakes
- Porridge
- Wholewheat Pasta
- Corn Pasta
- Popcorn
- Potato Flour
- Quinoa
- Rice Flour
- Wild Rice
- Rye
- Rye Bread
- Rye Crackers
- Rye Flour
- Tapioca
- Triticale
- Wholewheat Bread
- Wholewheat Flour
- Biscuits
- Crackers
- Cakes
- Pastry

STARCHY VEGETABLES (ALL ALKALINE-FORMING)

+ Potato
+ Sweet Potato

+ Sweetcorn
+ Taro
+ Yams

SWEETENINGS

+ Blackstrap Molasses
- Organic Unblended Honey
- Fructose Powder
  (fruit sugar)

- Real Maple Syrup
- Carob Spread

- Crystallized Ginger

Fruit (See Day Nine, page 58)

Make fruit a frequent and fundamental part of your food combining diet, but eat it separately from proteins and starches.

Here are some suggestions:

+ Apples
+ Yellow Apricots
+ Hunza Apricots
+ Banana
+ Blackberries
+ Blackcurrants
+ Blueberries
+ Boysenberries
+ Carambola
+ Cherries
+ Clementines
+ Cumquat
+ Currants
+ Dates
+ Figs
+ Grapefruit
+ Grapes
+ Guava
+ Huckleberries
+ Jackfruit
+ Kiwi Fruit
+ Lemons
+ Lillypilly Fruits
+ Limes
+ Loganberries
+ Lychees
+ Mandarins

+ Mangoes
+ Medlars
+ Melons[1]
+ Mulberries
+ Nectarines
+ Olives (black only)
+ Papaya (Paw-paw)
+ Passionfruit
+ Peaches
+ Pears
+ Pepino
+ Persimmon (Date Plum)
+ Pineapple
+ Pitahaya (Cactus Fruit)
+ Plantain
+ Pomegranate
+ Raisins
+ Raspberries
+ Redcurrants
+ Sapodilla
+ Satsumas
+ Star Apple
+ Strawberries
+ Sultanas
+ Tangelo
+ Tangerines

As explained in Day Nine, page 62, fruit and its juices should be taken on an empty stomach.

[1] Melons are a special case. They are digested very quickly indeed and do not mix well with anything else at all — so for best results eat them entirely on their own and leave a good 15 minutes between courses if you choose melon as a starter.

Herbs and Spices

Herbs and spices are classed as neutral 'mix with anything' foods, happy with either proteins or starches and fabulously flavourful additions to salad and vegetable dishes too. There are plenty to choose from and many which you can grow in the herb garden or in pots on the kitchen windowsill.

HERBS

+ Angelica
+ Basil
+ Bay Leaf
+ Borage
+ Chervil
+ Chives
+ Coriander (Cilantro)
+ Dill
+ Fennel
+ Fenugreek
+ Lemon Balm
+ Lemon Grass
+ Lemon Verbena
+ Lovage
+ Marjoram
+ Mint
+ Oregano
+ Parsley
+ Rosemary
+ Sage
+ Salad Burnet
+ Savory
+ Shiso
+ Tansy
+ Tarragon
+ Thyme

SPICES

- Allspice
- Cayenne (Chilli)
- Cinnamon
- Cloves
- Cumin
- Ginger
- Liquorice
- Mustard
- Paprika
- Tumeric

Spices add extra flavour to many dishes but can be a source of stomach irritation if taken in large quantities, so use them sparingly.

Nuts and Seeds

Nuts and seeds are also classed as 'mix with anything' foods. However, nuts can be difficult for some people to digest. If this is the case, try eating them either on their own as snacks or with salads only. Always chew nuts and seeds as thoroughly as possible.

NUTS

+ Almonds
+ Brazil Nuts
- Candle Nuts
- Cashew Nuts
- Coconut
- Filberts (Hazelnuts)
- Water Chestnuts

- Pecan Nuts
- Pine Nuts
- Pistachios
- Tiger Nuts
- Walnuts
- Macadamia Nuts

SEEDS

+ Caraway Seeds
+ Celery Seeds
+ Dill Seeds
+ Fennel Seeds
+ Fenugreek Seeds

+ Linseeds
+ Poppy Seeds
+ Pumpkin Seeds (Pepitas)
+ Sesame Seeds
+ Sunflower Seeds

Vegetables

Vegetables are a vital part of any healthy eating programme and are particularly important 'combining foods' since they mix happily with proteins or starches.

Neutral 'mix-with-anything' vegetables are rich in dietary fibre, vitamins and minerals and low in fat. Include as much variety as possible in your diet and, if there is one vegetable or salad food that you don't particularly like, replace it with another. Try to have at least one portion of salad and a good mix of three or four vegetables every day.

Here are some suggestions:

+ Jerusalem or Globe Artichokes
- Asparagus
+ Aubergine (Eggplant)
+ Avocado (a 'vegetable fruit')
+ Bamboo shoots

+ Batavian endive (Escarole)
+ Bean sprouts
+ Beet greens
+ Raw Beetroot
+ Belgian endive (chicory)
+ Broccoli
+ Brussels sprouts
+ White- and Dark-leaved Cabbage
+ Calabrese

+ Capsicums, Red, Green or Yellow (Bell) Peppers
+ Carrots
+ Cassava
+ Cauliflower

+ Eggplant (Aubergine)
+ Kale (Collard greens)
+ Kohlrabi

+ Leek
+ Lettuce – all kinds and all colours

+ Mangetout (Snow Peas)
+ Mushrooms
+ Mustard and Cress
+ Nettles
+ Organic Sea Vegetables
+ Okra
+ Onion

+ Peas
+ Radishes (also known as watercress with knobs on!)

+ Romaine
+ Spinach
+ Spring Onions (Scallions)
+ Sprouted seeds

+ Cauliflower greens
+ Celery and Celeriac
+ Choko (or Chayote,
  the vegetable pear)
+ Courgette (Zucchini)
+ Cress
+ Cucumber
+ Dandelion greens

+ Sugar Snap Peas
+ Swede (Rutabaga)

+ Swiss Chard
+ Raw Tomatoes
+ Turnips
+ Turnip greens
+ Watercress

Easy Reference Chart

Keep this chart in the kitchen or with your shopping list.

You can mix the *Proteins* in **COLUMN A** with
  anything from **COLUMN B**
or mix the *Starches* in **COLUMN C** with anything
  from **COLUMN B**
but *don't* mix **COLUMN A** with **COLUMN C**

COLUMN A	**COLUMN B**	**COLUMN C**
Proteins	*Mix With Anything*	*Starches*
Fish	All vegetables except potatoes	Potatoes and sweet potatoes
Shellfish	All salads	All grains including oats, pasta, brown rice, rye, maize and millet
Free-range eggs	Seeds	
Free-range poultry	Nuts	Biscuits and cakes
Lamb	Herbs	Bread and crackers
Rabbit	Cream	Pastry
Cheese	Butter	Sugar and sweets
Yoghurt	Olive oil	Honey
Soya beans and all soya products	Spreading fats	Maple syrup

Notes:

1 Nuts are very concentrated foods and for some people are difficult to digest. Whilst they can be mixed in small quantities with other foods, ideally they should be eaten on their own as snacks or combined with vegetables or salads. If they have caused you discomfort in the past, it may have been the *combination* rather than the nuts themselves which upset you. Indeed, some of the earliest food combining books suggested that nuts should not be mixed with proteins or starches at all. Nuts do add extra nourishment and variety to so many dishes, however.

2 Fruits are not listed in the above chart because they are more easily digested when eaten separately from proteins and starches. It's fine to brighten up a savoury salad with fresh fruit as long as no proteins or starches are included.

3 Pulses are not included in the columns above because food combining law treats them as a 'special case'. They mix well with salads and vegetables but not with other proteins or starches.

4 All food combining experts agree that milk does not combine well with other foods. It can be an aggravating allergen, responsible for digestive discomfort, bowel disorders, catarrh and sinus problems. Use it in small amounts in beverages if necessary and, otherwise, keep it to a minimum. It is extremely unlikely that you will suffer calcium deficiency by not having milk since, contrary to popular belief, milk calcium is not well absorbed. For more information on milk, see 'Low Energy Foods', page 109. By its very nature, food combining provides plentiful calcium from other sources including yoghurt, cheese, grains, nuts, fish and vegetables without the need for large amounts of cow's milk.

Recipes

―――――――――― ❧ ――――――――――

To help you plan your food combining meals, the recipes are divided under Protein, Starch and Alkaline headings. From this section you'll be able to create your own weekly menus; you'll notice that some of the fruit and yoghurt breakfast recipes would also make excellent desserts.

All you need to do is to ensure you have one protein-based meal, one starch-based meal and one completely alkaline-forming meal each day, to ensure you give your body the perfect balance of alkaline-forming and acid-forming foods. Or if you prefer to vary the 'one of each' rule, remember that you can, in fact, have two starch and one alkaline *or* two alkaline and one starch *or* one protein and two alkaline, *or even* two starch and one protein meals per day – although during the course of a week you should aim to have seven of each, if possible. And don't forget the most important rule of all – to enjoy your food! These recipes will help you to enjoy food combining as a delicious new way of eating.

You can compose impressive menu plans for special meals or entertaining and vary them according to the season or your own preferences, as long as you remember not to mix protein and starch dishes at the same meal. For example:

Avocado and Spinach Salad (p.163), Salmon Parcel
   with Steamed Vegetable Medley (pp.141, 163),
   (wait an hour) Summer Fruit Platter (p.163).
Celery and Cashew Nut Soup (p.166), Chicken
   Provençal with Mixed Green Salad (pp.139, 160),
   (wait an hour) Exotic Fruit Platter (p.163).
Avocado Dip with Crudités (p.146), Baked
   Ratatouille (p.143), Apricot Bake (p.167)
Melon Cocktail (p.159, wait 15 minutes before
   serving next course), Avocado and Spinach Salad
   (p.163), Sunburst Rice (p.149)

It's preferable if you are food combining properly to
wait longer than an hour between eating fruit and
eating other foods, but obviously you can bend the rules
a little if you are entertaining. Alternatively, you could
serve the courses in a different order, having, say, Exotic
Fruit Platter followed by Celery and Cashew Nut Soup
followed by Chicken Provençal – why not try it!

Some of the recipes include tomatoes; raw tomatoes
are alkaline-forming and can be combined with either
protein or starch. Cooking tomatoes, however, can not
only destroy their vitamin C but also increases their
acidity, making them incompatible with starches. You
may find tomatoes easier to digest – and improved in
flavour – if you skin them. Try the following method:

Put the tomatoes in a heat-proof glass jug and pour
just-boiled water over them. Leave them submerged
for 25 seconds, then pour away the water and take the
tomatoes out of the jug. Take a thin slice off the very
top of each one and you will find that the skin comes
away easily.

A vegetable that appears in some of the recipes is raw onion: if you find the flavour overwhelming then simply omit the onion from the recipe.

Remember to use organically grown fruit and vegetables wherever possible; if these are unobtainable, then all fruit and vegetables should be peeled or thoroughly scrubbed clean before use.

All the recipes serve one person unless otherwise stated.

Protein Recipes

❧

Protein Breakfasts

BANANA SWIRL

Blend together in a liquidizer or food processor one ripe banana with the contents of 1 small tub of plain live yoghurt, 1 teaspoonful of clear honey and 1 dessertspoonful of ground almonds.

YOGHURT SMOOTHIE

Place the contents of 1 small tub of plain, live yoghurt in a serving glass and drizzle over 1 teaspoonful clear honey — choose a cold-pressed honey from your health food shop for added flavour.

YOGHURT CRUNCH

Place the contents of 1 small tub of plain, live yoghurt in a serving glass and top with a tablespoonful of chopped hazelnuts, flaked almonds, sunflower seeds or linseeds, or any combination of the four.

POACHER'S PLATTER

Serve two poached free-range eggs with two halved, grilled tomatoes garnished with chopped parsley.

As this is a *protein* breakfast, don't be tempted to have it with bread.

SCRAMBLED DELIGHT

Scramble one or two free-range eggs with one or two dessertspoonsful of cream (*not* milk) and a dash of filtered water. Serve with chopped flat mushrooms softened in a little butter or olive oil with a dash of lemon juice and freshly ground black pepper.

Again, you should not have bread or any other starch accompaniment with this meal.

Protein Main Courses

Chicken Dishes

CHICKEN AND COURGETTE (ZUCCHINI) KEBABS

Ingredients
1 free-range chicken breast, skinned and boned
1 tablespoonful extra virgin olive oil
1 teaspoonful fresh lemon juice
freshly ground black pepper to taste
sprigs of fresh tarragon or thyme
1 courgette (zucchini)
½ green (bell) pepper
4 or 5 cherry tomatoes

Cut the chicken breast into inch cubes and marinade for 30 minutes in the olive oil and lemon juice, freshly ground black pepper and a few chopped sprigs of tarragon or thyme. Thickly slice the courgette (zucchini) and cut the green (bell) pepper into inch cubes. Thread alternately the chicken cubes, courgette (zucchini) slices, pepper cubes and tomatoes onto a skewer. Brush with the marinade and grill (broil) for 15–20 minutes, turning occasionally, until the chicken is tender. Serve with a Mixed Red Salad (p.161).

TARRAGON BAKED CHICKEN

Ingredients
1 free-range chicken breast
1 dessertspoonful extra virgin olive oil
sprig of fresh tarragon

Brush the chicken breast with the olive oil and place in a covered baking dish with the tarragon. Bake at 200°C/400°F/Gas Mark 6 for 30 minutes, baste with juices, remove cover and cook for a further 10 minutes. Serve hot with a side salad.

CHICKEN PROVENÇAL

Ingredients
2 shallots, finely chopped
1 clove of garlic, crushed
1 dessertspoonful extra virgin olive oil
2 medium skinned, chopped tomatoes
½ green (bell) pepper, sliced
4 brown mushrooms, sliced
1 chicken quarter or part-boned chicken breast, free range
1 teaspoonful chopped fresh basil

Gently sauté the shallots and garlic in the olive oil for two minutes. Stir in the tomatoes, green pepper and mushrooms. Bring to a simmer then place in a casserole dish with the chicken quarter/breast and the basil. Bake at 190°C/375°F/Gas Mark 5 for 1¼ hours. Serve with lightly cooked green vegetables.

SKEWERED SPICED CHICKEN

Ingredients
1 free-range chicken breast
½ inch (1cm) cube root ginger, peeled and grated
1 garlic clove, finely chopped

¼ teaspoonful ground cumin seeds
3 tablespoonfuls plain, live yoghurt
knob of butter

Cut the chicken breast into inch cubes and place in a
bowl. Mix the root ginger with the garlic, ground cumin
seeds and yoghurt. Press through a sieve and pour onto
the diced chicken. Cover and chill for at least 2 hours
before threading loosely onto a skewer, brushing with
a knob of melted butter and baking at the oven's hottest
temperature for seven minutes, turning once. Served
with Grilled Vegetable Kebabs or Steamed Vegetable
Medley (pp.164, 163).

CHICKEN AND CASHEW NUT STIR FRY

Ingredients
1 tablespoonful extra virgin olive oil
1 free-range chicken breast, skinned and cut into
    inch (2.5cm) strips
½ leek, finely shredded
1 carrot, grated
½ red (bell) pepper, finely sliced
handful of mung beansprouts
handful of cashew nuts
1 tablespoonful filtered water
1 teaspoonful soy sauce

Heat the olive oil in a wok or large frying pan and stir
in the chicken strips. Cook until just tender, remove
from pan and set aside. In the same pan stir in the
shredded leek, grated carrot and sliced red pepper.
Cook for 2 minutes, then add the mung beansprouts,
cashew nuts, water and soy sauce. Cook 2 minutes
more, stir in the chicken and serve.

SALMON PARCEL

Ingredients
1 salmon steak
knob of butter
sprigs of fresh dill or tarragon, to taste
1 tablespoonful dry white wine, to taste

Place the salmon steak on a square double thickness greaseproof paper, add the knob of butter and, if liked, a few sprigs of fresh dill or tarragon and the dry white wine. Seal the edges, place on a baking tray and bake in a pre-heated oven at 375°F/190°C/Gas Mark 5 for 25 minutes. Serve with the Steamed Vegetable Medley (p.163).

MEDITERRANEAN FISH BAKE

Ingredients
1 fillet firm white fish, such as cod or haddock
2 shallots, chopped
1 dessertspoonful extra virgin olive oil
½ green and ½ red (bell) pepper, sliced
8oz/225g tomatoes, skinned and chopped
sprigs fresh marjoram, chopped

Cut the fish into 1 inch (2.5cm) cubes. Lightly sauté the shallots in the olive oil for 2 minutes, then stir in the green and red pepper. Add the tomatoes and a few sprigs of marjoram. Bring to the boil, then carefully stir in the fish, cover, and reduce heat to simmer for 20 minutes. Serve with Steamed Vegetable Medley or a Mixed Green Salad (pp.163, 160).

CHINESE-STYLE STEAMED FISH

Ingredients
1 fillet of plaice or sole
1 teaspoonful peeled and finely grated root ginger
1 spring onion (scallion), finely chopped
1 tablespoonful light soy sauce

Place the fish in a steamer (or on a plate) and scatter
the ginger on top. Steam for 5 minutes, then sprinkle
on the spring onion (scallion) and soy sauce. Serve with
Stir Fry Vegetables (p.164).

TROUT BAKED WITH ALMONDS

Ingredients
1 trout
juice of half a lemon
1 tablespoonful flaked almonds

Pat the trout dry and brush the inside with the lemon
juice. Scatter the flaked almonds onto a plate and toss
the trout to cover lightly both sides. Bake on a sheet
of greaseproof paper at 230°C/450°F/Gas Mark 8 for
6 minutes each side, until cooked through. Serve with
Mixed Green Salad (p.160).

PLAICE AND PRAWN ROLL UPS

Ingredients
1 large plaice fillet, skinned
knob of butter
1 shallot, finely chopped

2 large field mushrooms
1 tablespoonful peeled prawns
sprigs of fresh dill or parsley, chopped
⅛ pint/75ml filtered water
1 tablespoonful dry white wine

Cut the plaice fillet lengthwise into two strips. Melt the butter in a pan and sauté the shallot with the mushrooms, until the mushrooms are soft. Remove from heat and stir in the prawns and most of the dill or parsley (reserving some for a garnish). Divide mixture into two and spread on top of each piece of plaice. Roll up loosely and secure with cocktail sticks. Place in a buttered, shallow ovenproof dish and pour the water mixed with dry white wine over. Cover and bake at 200°C/400°F/Gas Mark 6 for 20 minutes. Serve garnished with herbs, with Steamed Vegetable Medley (p.163).

Cheese Dishes

BAKED RATATOUILLE

This recipe makes a double portion – serve the ratatouille plain, either hot or chilled, on the first day, then baked with the savoury topping on the following day. The savoury topping makes this a protein dish, so omit the topping if you'd prefer an alkaline meal.

Ingredients
1 tablespoonful extra virgin olive oil
2 baby onions, chopped
1 garlic clove, crushed
1 medium-sized aubergine (eggplant), cut into ½ inch (1 cm) chunks

½ red and ½ green (bell) pepper, sliced
1 small courgette (zucchini), sliced
2 medium tomatoes, skinned and chopped
1 teaspoonful chopped fresh basil
For the savoury topping:
1 large free-range egg
1 small tub plain natural yoghurt
1oz/25g farmhouse Cheddar cheese, grated

Heat the olive oil in a pan with the onion and garlic. Cook for 2 minutes, then stir in the aubergine (eggplant) and cook for a further 2 minutes. Then stir in the red and green (bell) peppers, courgette (zucchini), tomatoes and basil. Bring to the boil, then cover and simmer for 25 minutes.

To bake: Place the ratatouille in an ovenproof dish. Beat together the free range egg and yoghurt, pour the mixture over the ratatouille and sprinkle the grated Cheddar cheese on top. Bake for 25 minutes at 190°C/375°F/Gas Mark 5 until set.

CREAMY CAULIFLOWER CHEESE

Ingredients
2 baby onions
1 small leek
1 tablespoon olive oil
1 small cauliflower
1 tablespoon filtered water
1 tablespoon white wine
2oz grated cheese (your favourite)
2 tablespoons double cream
salt and freshly ground black pepper to taste

Chop the onions and leek and sauté them in a pan with the olive oil until tender. Break the cauliflower into small florets and add to the pan with the water. Put the lid on tight and simmer until tender (about 10 minutes). Shake pan frequently to prevent sticking. Add the white wine, cheese, double cream and seasoning. Stir for a further minute.

If you are on your own, serve half this amount today and keep the rest for tomorrow.

The cheese makes this a protein meal, but you could leave it out if you wanted to have an alkaline-forming meal instead.

CHEESEY OMELETTE

Ingredients
2 medium-sized free-range eggs
1 tablespoon filtered water
sprigs of thyme and parsley, finely chopped
freshly ground black pepper
1 dessertspoonful olive oil
1 baby onion, finely chopped
3 shiitake mushrooms, finely chopped
1oz/25g farmhouse Cheddar cheese, grated

Lightly beat the eggs together with the water, thyme and parsley and some freshly ground black pepper. Preheat a grill (broiler). Heat the olive oil in an omelette pan and gently sauté the chopped onion and mushrooms until the juices run. Pour the beaten egg mixture over the sautéeing vegetables and cook quickly until the mixture is just set. Sprinkle the grated cheese on top and place under the heated grill (broiler) to finish cooking. Serve with a Mixed Green Salad (p.160).

FETA CHEESE SALAD

Ingredients
2 ripe tomatoes, skinned and sliced
½ cucumber, thinly sliced
a few onion rings
2oz/50g feta cheese, diced
a few black olives
sprig of fresh basil, chopped

Arrange the tomatoes on a dish with the thinly sliced cucumber, onion rings, diced feta cheese and olives. Pour over a little Olive Oil and Cider Vinegar Dressing (p.160) and garnish with basil.

AVOCADO DIP WITH CRUDITÉS

Ingredients
½ an avocado
2oz/50g curd cheese
dash of fresh lemon juice
pieces of raw vegetables, e.g. cauliflower florets, green and red (bell) pepper slices, or courgette (zucchini), carrot, cucumber or celery batons

Purée the avocado with the curd cheese and a dash of fresh lemon juice. Serve with pieces of raw vegetables of your choice.

Starch Recipes

❧

Starch Breakfasts

IRISH BREAKFAST

Serve wholewheat soda bread, sliced and buttered, with honey.

ITALIAN BREAKFAST

Bake or warm thoroughly Italian ciabatta bread, either plain or flavoured, and serve with butter or a little sugar-free' fruit preserve. Ciabatta freezes well, so if you're on your own break the loaf into pieces to be frozen separately.

MIDDLE EASTERN BREAKFAST

Split a wholewheat pitta bread, toast and serve buttered and spread with nut butter, cold-pressed honey or a little sugar-free fruit preserve.

HONEYED PORRIDGE

Stir ½ cup organic oatmeal or oatbran into 1½ cups of water and bring to the boil, stirring constantly. Simmer for 2 minutes, then stir in 1 teaspoonful speciality cold-pressed dark honey (from a health food shop) and 1 tablespoonful sultanas.

HOMEMADE MUESLI

This is the tried and tested Muesli recipe that appeared in *The Food Combining Diet*; I have found this to be the most delicious combination. The amount of starch in 1 tablespoon of oatmeal or oatbran is very small and therefore will mix quite comfortably with the apple.

Soak 1 level tablespoonful oatmeal or oatbran overnight in the refrigerator in 4 tablespoonsful filtered water and 2 tablespoonsful apple juice (not carbonated). In the morning, grate 1 eating apple into 1 tablespoonful fresh lemon juice and mix in the soaked oats, and 1 level tablespoonful each of the following: unblanched grated almonds, grated Brazil nuts, raisins, linseeds, pumpkin seeds and sunflower seeds. Serve with a little diluted cream.

Food Combining Guidelines: This delicious mixture is moist enough to eat without adding extra liquid. The addition of large amounts of milk to cereals is not recommended, since milk is a protein and most cereals are starch-based, thereby making them incompatible. However, if at first you find it difficult to adjust, then add a little diluted organic raw milk or a small amount of diluted cream.

Starch Main Courses

Rice

SUNBURST RICE

Ingredients
1 tablespoonful chopped onion
1 stick celery, finely sliced
1 dessertspoonful extra virgin olive oil
3oz/75g long grain brown rice
7fl oz/210ml filtered water
1 bay leaf
1 medium-sized carrot, finely grated
1 dessertspoonful chopped parsley
1 tablespoonful sunflower seeds

Sauté the onion and celery together in the olive oil for 2 minutes. Stir in the long grain brown rice, water and bay leaf. Bring to the boil, cover and simmer for 20–30 minutes, or until the rice is tender. Fork in the grated carrot, chopped parsley and scatter the sunflower seeds on top.

SPICED VEGETABLE PILAO

Ingredients
1 tablespoonful extra virgin olive oil
¼ teaspoonful cumin seeds
1 shallot, chopped
1 carrot, finely chopped
a few cauliflower florets
3oz/75g brown basmati rice

7 fl oz/210ml filtered water
1oz/25g cashew nuts

Heat the olive oil in a pan and stir in the cumin seeds.
Add the shallot, chopped carrot and cauliflower florets.
Stir well and cook for 1 minute. Stir in the rice and add
the water. Bring to the boil, then reduce the heat and
simmer for 25–30 minutes or until the rice is tender
and the liquid absorbed (check occasionally to ensure
mixture is not drying out). Finally, fork in the cashew
nuts.

VEGETABLE RICE

Ingredients
1 tablespoonful extra virgin olive oil
1 tablespoonful finely chopped onion
1 garlic clove, crushed (optional)
2½oz/65g long grain brown rice
½oz/13g wild rice
1 courgette (zucchini), sliced
2 tablespoonsful sweetcorn kernels
½ red (bell) pepper, diced
7 fl oz/210ml filtered water
½ teaspoonful soy sauce

Heat the olive oil in a pan and stir in the onion and
garlic (optional) and cook for 1 minute. Add the rice
and stir in well. Then add the courgette (zucchini),
sweetcorn kernels, diced red (bell) pepper, water and
soy sauce. Bring to the boil, cover and simmer for
20–30 minutes until the rice is tender.

MUSHROOM-TOPPED POTATO

Ingredients
1 baking potato
knob of butter
1 shallot, chopped
3oz/75g mushrooms (preferably chestnut), finely
   chopped
sprig of fresh thyme, finely chopped
1 dessertspoonful single cream
freshly ground black pepper to taste

Scrub and prick the potato and bake at 200°C/
400°F/Gas Mark 6 for 1–1¼ hours until soft. Melt the
butter and sauté together the chopped shallot,
mushrooms and thyme. When the mushrooms are soft,
stir in the cream and season with freshly ground black
pepper. Split the potato almost in half lengthwise and
pour the mushroom mixture on top. Serve with a
Mixed Green Salad (p.160).

POTATO BAKE

Ingredients
1 baking potato, cut into fine slices
1 shallot, sliced
1 carrot, finely grated
6oz/175g fresh (or 4oz/100g frozen) spinach, cooked
   and drained
¼ pint/150ml filtered water
1 tablespoonful single cream
pinch of mixed dried herbs

Layer the potato slices in a buttered dish alternately with the sliced shallot, grated carrot, and cooked spinach. Pour over the water and cream mixed with the dried herbs and cover. Bake in a preheated oven at 190°C/375°F/Gas Mark 5 for an hour until the potatoes are tender. Serve with warmed wholewheat soda bread.

BAKED POTATO

Remember that a plain, baked jacket potato makes a simple, filling and tasty meal. Serve with a Mixed Green Salad (p.160) — *not* with cheese!

Pasta Meals

If you decide to use fresh pasta in any of these recipes, it's worth remembering that fresh pasta cooks much more quickly than the dried variety.

SPAGHETTI WITH OLIVE OIL AND GARLIC

Ingredients
3oz/75g wholewheat spaghetti
1 tablespoonful extra virgin olive oil
1 garlic clove, finely chopped
1 tablespoonful finely chopped parsley

Plunge the spaghetti into a pan of boiling water and cook until nearly tender. Heat the olive oil in a separate pan large enough to hold the pasta, and sauté the garlic until lightly golden. Drain the pasta when cooked and add to the oil and garlic. Cook for a few minutes, stirring constantly and stir in the chopped parsley. Serve at once with Mixed Green Salad (p.160).

PASTA PRIMAVERA

Ingredients
a dozen baby corn
1 carrot, cut into fine matchsticks
1 small courgette (zucchini), finely sliced
2 runner beans
handful of mangetout (snowpeas)
2oz/50g wholewheat pasta shells (or pasta of your choice)
fresh herbs, e.g. parsley, chives, thyme or tarragon

Blanch the vegetables by plunging them into boiling water briefly so that their crispness is retained, then cool them in cold water, and drain thoroughly. Mix the drained vegetables in Olive Oil and Cider Vinegar Dressing (p.160) and then cook the pasta shells until *al dente* or just tender and stir into the vegetables with a mixture of finely chopped fresh herbs.

NIÇOISE SALAD

Ingredients
2oz/50g wholewheat pasta twists
1 large ripe tomato, skinned and sliced
½ red (bell) pepper, finely sliced
1 inch (2.5cm) piece of cucumber, cut into fine sticks
2oz/50g French beans, cut into 1 inch (2.5cm) pieces

a few black olives
sprigs of fresh basil

Prepare some Olive Oil and Cider Vinegar Dressing
(p.160). Cook the pasta twists until *al dente* or just
tender and stir into the tomato, pepper and cucumber.
Blanch the French beans and stir them in to the rest·
of the vegetables. Toss the mixture in a bowl with the
dressing. Garnish with the olives and sprigs of basil.

SAPCOTE SOUP

Ingredients
2 large or 4 small leeks
4 shallots
1 garlic clove (if liked)
2 tablespoons extra virgin olive oil
1 head fennel
2 large carrots
1 small turnip
1 small parsnip
1 large flat mushroom
2 oz brown fusilli bucati (pasta twists)
6 sun-dried tomatoes
salt and freshly ground black pepper
1 tablespoon chopped fresh parsley

Finely chop the leeks, shallots and garlic and fry in the
olive oil in a large pan until softened. Dice all the other
vegetables and add to the pan. (Do not add the
tomatoes, herbs or pasta at this stage.) Cover with
water, bring to the boil and simmer for fifteen minutes.
Add the pasta and cook until the pasta is tender (about

five to six minutes). Now chop the tomatoes and add to the mixture. Add a sprinkling of salt and black pepper, garnish with the parsley and, if liked, serve with buttered ciabatta or wholewheat pitta bread.

Author's note: This tasty and filling starch 'soup' is a meal in itself. My thanks to a very dear friend, Hazel Sapcote, for providing the recipe.

Sandwich Fillings (Starch Meals)

All breads, whether wholewheat, soda, pumpernickel or pitta, are starches, and should not be combined with proteins, so all the fillings listed here are alkaline-forming.

Avoid additive-laden, 'squashy' supermarket breads, whether brown or white, and instead try your hand at baking your own, or look out for traditional breads made with stoneground, organic flour. The closer the texture of the loaf and the firmer it is, the less yeast and gluten it is likely to contain; both yeast and gluten are common allergens, especially if taken in large amounts.

Spread breads with butter or a top-quality vegetable margarine made with oils that have not been hydrogenated or 'hardened' during processing (see Resources).

Try these fillings for a change:

- Avocado: half an avocado, roughly mashed
- Watercress and Tomato: watercress sprigs with skinned, sliced tomato
- Carrot: coarsely grated carrot, chopped walnuts and raisins
- Green Salad: shredded lettuce, sliced cucumber, diced green pepper and mustard and cress
- Nut Butter: nut butter (not peanut) and alfalfa sprouts
- Celery and Carrot: chopped celery, grated carrot and flaked almonds
- Salad Sprouts: alfalfa sprouts, skinned, sliced tomato and sliced cucumber

- Chip Butty: sauté sliced potatoes in a few tablespoonsful of extra virgin olive oil, turn during cooking to brown evenly, drain and sprinkle with sea salt, lo-salt or sodium-free salt replacer and sandwich together. (Both potatoes and bread are starchy foods.)
- Pitta Bread: made with wholewheat flour makes an ideal 'pocket' for a savoury salad filling. Choose from shredded lettuce, cucumber, skinned sliced tomatoes, grated carrot, olives or avocado.

Open Sandwiches are a less transportable alternative to conventional sandwiches, but made with continental-style pumpernickel breads are colourful and attractive. Try these:

- Sliced avocado and watercress sprigs
- Chopped chives, cherry tomatoes, olives, pine nuts and fresh basil

Starch Dessert

HOT CINNAMON CUSTARD

Ingredients
1 tablespoon speciality honey
2 teaspoonsful powdered cinnamon
3 level tablespoonsful polenta (corn meal)
¼ cup milk
1 cup filtered water

Mix together the honey, cinnamon and polenta in a large heatproof bowl. In a pan, heat the milk and water to boiling point (but do not boil) then remove from heat and pour slowly over the mixture, stirring until smooth. Return to the pan and stir until the texture thickens to a smooth custard. Serve drizzled with extra honey if desired.

Alkaline Recipes

_____ ❧ _____

Alkaline Breakfasts

MELON COCKTAIL
Choose a mixture of galia, cantaloupe and honeydew melon, cut into chunks and serve together.

FRESH PINEAPPLE AND KIWI
Cut a chunk of fresh pineapple, peel, core and cut into slices and arrange on a plate with a peeled and thinly sliced kiwi fruit.

JUNGLE FRESH
Choose either papaya or mango, peel and slice finely.

STUFFED PEARS
Cut two small pears in half, cut out the core and fill with raisins and flaked almonds.

DRIED FRUIT COMPOTE
Choose from dried apricots, hunza apricots, prunes, figs, peaches, pears, apple slices, large raisins and place in a pan with just enough water to cover. Add a cinnamon stick and 2 cloves, bring to the boil then turn off the heat and leave in the pan for 8 hours or overnight to soften. Serve as it is or with plain live yoghurt.

Alkaline Main Courses

Salads

There is a wonderful variety of different salad ingredients available today, so there's no need to stick to just plain lettuce and tomato. Make up vibrant mixtures based on fresh vegetables and other salad ingredients using more or less of each, as suggested below, to suit your own taste. These salads are designed to be eaten as light, alkaline-forming meals in their own right, but the Mixed Green Salad, Mixed Red Salad, Green Zinger and Avocado and Spinach Salad could all be served as accompaniments to either protein or starch-based dishes too.

Dark-coloured lettuce is more nourishing than the paler varieties, so look out for more unusual lettuces like oak leaf or radicchio.

For speed and simplicity, these salads can be served with olive oil and either lemon juice or cider vinegar; experiment with the quantities to suit yourself. Otherwise you can try out different recipes for dressings, or use plain live yoghurt, which is alkaline-forming.

Remember to wash all salad ingredients thoroughly before use.

MIXED GREEN SALAD

Choose any lettuce — cos, webb's, little gem, round, iceberg, oak leaf or lollo rosso — as a base and then add any of the following: endive, watercress, young spinach, sliced green pepper, sliced cucumber, chopped celery, spring onions (scallions), mustard and cress. Toss in Olive Oil and Lemon Dressing (see above) and garnish with chopped chives.

THE MARSDEN SALAD

This salad, repeated here from *The Food Combining Diet*, has proved to be a great success, so if you haven't tried it before now is the time to do so. It is an excellent lymph and liver detoxifier.

Choose as many as possible of the following ingredients: grated raw beetroot; celery; carrot; dandelion leaves (*not* picked on a busy roadside where they will have been exposed to pollution); watercress; Spanish onion; sprouted fenugreek seeds; sprouted alfalfa seeds; 1 garlic clove (crushed); 1 teaspoon chopped chives.

To make this salad into a starch meal add 1 cup of cooked brown rice.

Tear all the leaves into small pieces and mix with the rice (if using), seeds, chives, crushed garlic and dress with olive oil and lemon juice.

If you want to use this with a protein meal don't forget to omit the rice.

MIXED RED SALAD

Combine radicchio, cherry tomatoes, sliced red (bell) pepper, thinly sliced red skinned onion and radishes in Olive Oil and Lemon Dressing (above) flavoured with freshly chopped basil.

GRAPE AND WALNUT SALAD

Shred some dark lettuce leaves of your choice (e.g. oak leaf lettuce) and mix with fresh coriander or chervil (if available), a handful of walnuts, a handful of seedless grapes and small cubes of ricotta cheese.

If you omit the cheese (protein) this salad will mix happily with any other meal.

COLESLAW

Mix together finely shredded white cabbage, grated carrot, grated onion, raisins, grated skinned eating apple, tossed in a teaspoonful of lemon juice and bind with plain live yoghurt.

RED CABBAGE CRUNCH

Combine finely shredded red cabbage with chopped celery, sliced cucumber, sprigs of watercress and a handful of walnuts. Garnish with chopped parsley.

GREEN ZINGER

Have ready a pan of fast boiling water and plunge into the pan for 2–5 minutes a combination of trimmed French beans cut into 1 inch (2.5cm) lengths, small florets of cauliflower, sliced courgette (zucchini) and some mangetout (snowpeas) or sugar snap peas. Drain thoroughly and toss at once into Olive Oil and Lemon Dressing (above) flavoured with freshly chopped chives.

AVOCADO AND SPINACH SALAD

Trim and tear roughly a good handful of young spinach leaves. Arrange on a plate and top with half a sliced avocado, cherry tomatoes, a few cucumber slices and a tablespoonful of sunflower seeds or cashew nuts. Serve with Olive Oil and Cider Vinegar (above) if liked.

SUMMER FRUIT PLATTER

Arrange a finely sliced peach or nectarine on a plate with some strawberries, grapes, and a sliced banana.

EXOTIC FRUIT PLATTER

Peel and thinly slice a quarter of a mango and arrange with peeled, sliced papaya, pineapple and kiwi fruit.

Vegetable Dishes

STEAMED VEGETABLE MEDLEY

Cook the vegetables in a stainless steel steamer, or using the pan method: put an inch of water in a pan and bring to the boil, adding the vegetables in turn and clamping the lid on tightly between each one. Start with the longest cooking vegetable and finish with the quickest. Here is a rough guide: root vegetables (15–20 minutes), leeks and runner beans (12), baby sweetcorn and spinach (10), cauliflower (8), French beans (6–8), broccoli, carrots and cabbage (5), courgettes (zucchini, 3), mangetout (snowpeas, 2).

SUMMER STIR-FRY WITH SEEDS

Heat 1 dessertspoonful extra virgin olive oil in a wok or large frying pan. Stir in 1 carrot cut into fine matchsticks, ¼ green (bell) pepper, sliced, ¼ red (bell) pepper, sliced, 1 sliced courgette (zucchini) and a few baby sweetcorn. Cook for 4 minutes, then add 2oz/50g mung beansprouts, 2 teaspoonsful soy sauce, 1 tablespoonful filtered water and a dash of rice wine or dry sherry (optional). Cook for 2 minutes then stir in 1 tablespoonful each of sunflower and sesame seeds and 1 finely chopped spring onion (scallion) and serve.

WINTER STIR-FRY WITH NUTS

Proceed as above but use the following vegetables: ½ leek finely shredded, 1 carrot, cut into fine matchsticks, 2oz/50g swede, 2oz/50g curly kale, 2oz/50g sliced mushrooms, and in place of the seeds and spring onions (scallions) add 1oz/25g split almonds.

GRILLED VEGETABLE KEBABS

Thread onto a long skewer slices of courgette (zucchini), strips of green, red or yellow (bell) pepper, a few bay leaves, a quartered onion, and a few chunks of aubergine (eggplant). Brush thoroughly with extra virgin olive oil seasoned with freshly ground black pepper and chopped marjoram or oregano. Grill (broil) for 10–15 minutes, turning frequently, until just tender.

BAKED RED CABBAGE

Layer 4oz/100g shredded red cabbage in a buttered ovenproof dish with half a stick of celery, sliced, a small shallot, finely chopped, half an eating apple, diced and ½ oz/13g sultanas. Pour over 3fl oz/90ml filtered water, mixed with a dash of cider vinegar and a pinch each of ground cinnamon and ground coriander. Cover and bake for 45–50 minutes at 180°C/350°F/Gas Mark 4.

WINTER HOT POT LAYER

Arrange in alternate layers 4oz/100g swede, peeled and sliced, 1 small turnip, peeled and sliced, 1 carrot, scrubbed and sliced, half a leek, sliced and 2oz/50g button mushrooms. Pour over a good ¼ pt/150ml boiling water mixed with a teaspoonful soy sauce and ¼ teaspoonful cumin seeds. Cover and bake at 180°C/375°F/Gas Mark 4 for 1–1¼ hours.

CREAMY MUSHROOM SOUP

Makes a double portion. Melt ½ oz/13g butter in a large saucepan and stir in half a leek, chopped, and 6oz/75g button mushrooms, chopped. Cook for 2 minutes then add 3/4 pt/750ml filtered water, a bay leaf and a sprig of thyme. Bring to the boil, then simmer for 20 minutes. Remove the bay leaf and purée with 3 tablespoonsful single cream. Season, reheat and serve garnished with freshly chopped parsley.

CELERY AND CASHEW NUT SOUP

Makes a double portion. Melt ½ oz/13g butter in a large saucepan and sauté 2 chopped shallots for 2 minutes. Stir in 4 sticks of celery, chopped and cook for 2 minutes. Add a bay leaf, 1oz/25g cashew nut pieces and 3/4 pt/750ml filtered water. Bring to the boil then simmer for 30 minutes. Remove bay leaf and purée. Reheat and serve garnished with chopped celery leaves.

WINTER WARMER

Makes a double portion. Heat 1 dessertspoonful extra virgin olive oil with a crushed garlic clove (optional) and a small onion, chopped. Sauté for 2 minutes then stir in 1 carrot, scrubbed and chopped, 1 parsnip and 1 turnip, both peeled and chopped, a small leek, shredded, 3 tablespoonsful filtered water, ¼ teaspoonful mixed dried herbs, and bring to the boil, then simmer for 40 minutes. Stir in the florets of 1 head of broccoli (and the chopped stalk if it's tender) 5 minutes before serving, and if liked 1 tablespoonful sweetcorn kernels. Serve with chopped chives.

Alkaline Dessert

APRICOT BAKE

Ingredients
10 apricot halves (soaked overnight)
2 tablespoons reserved soaking liquid
1 tablespoon lemon juice
1 tablespoon butter
1 tablespoon ground almonds
1 tablespoon sesame seeds
1 tablespoon sunflower seeds
1 tablespoon soft dark brown sugar

Quickly blend the apricots with the reserved soaking liquid and lemon juice in a liquidizer, and spread the mixture on the base of a buttered dish. Mix together the butter and dry ingredients until they have a breadcrumb consistency, then spread over the apricots. Bake at 400°F/200°C/Gas Mark 6 for about 15 minutes, until golden brown. Serve with a little whipped cream or plain live yohurt.

References

Day Five, p.39

Colbin A. *Food and Healing* pp.73–80, 148–159. Ballantine Books, New York 1986.

Day Twenty-Eight, p.92

Blair S.N., Goodyear N.N., Gibbons L.W. et al. 'Physical fitness and incidence of hypertension in healthy normotensive men and women.' *Ann. Rev. Public Health* 1987;252:487–480.

Braverman E.R. 'Sports and Exercise: Nutritional Augmentation and Health Benefits.' *J. Orthom. Med.* 1991;6:191–201.

Caren L.D. 'Effects of exercise on the human immune system: does exercise influence susceptibility to infections?' *Bioscience* 1991;41:410–415.

Duncan J.J. et al. 'Women Walking For Health And Fitness: How Much Is Enough?' *J. Am. Med. Assoc.* 1991;266(23):3295–3299.

Frankel T. 'Walking may protect hips.' *Prevention* magazine 8 February 1990.

Lennox S.S., Bedell F.R., Stone A.A. 'The effect of exercise on normal mood.' *J. Psychosomatic Res.*

1990;34(6):629–636.

Leon A.S., Connett J., Jacobs D.R. et al. 'Leisure-time physical activity levels and risk of coronary heart disease and death. The Multiple Risk Factor International Trial.' *J. Am. Med. Assoc.* 1987;258:2388–2395.

McGuire R. 'Twice daily exercise may reduce hypertension.' *Medical Tribune* 27 June, 1991.

McLellan R. Article on rebounding. *The American Chiropractor*, June 1991 pp.10–14.

'*Low-Energy Foods*', pp.105–116

Halliwell, B. 'The Salt Sellers'. *The Food Magazine* July/Sept 1991 pp.14–15. Published by The Food Commission.

'Can diet products help you slim?' *The Food Magazine* July/Sept 1991 p.17. Published by The Food Commission.

'The Slimming Scandal'. *The Food Magazine* Feb/April 1992 pp.8–9. Published by The Food Commission.

Roberts H.J. 'Reactions attributed to aspartame-containing products: 551 cases.' *J. Appl. Nutrition* 1988;40:45–94.

'Orange Juice Fraud'. *The Food Magazine* April/June 1991 p.15. Published by The Food Commission.

Collins A.M. et al. 'Bovine milk, including pasteurized milk, contains antibodies directed against allergens of clinical importance to man.' *Int. Arch. Allergy Appl. Immunol.* 1991;96:362–367.

Ziegler E.E., Fomon S.J., Nelson S.E., Rebouche C.J., Edwards B.B., et al. 'Cow's milk feeding in infancy: further observations on blood loss from the gastrointestinal tract.' *J. Pediatr.* 1990;116:11–18.

Fernandes C.F., Shahani K.M. 'Lactose intolerance and its modulation with lactobacilli and other microbial supplements.' *J. Appl. Nutrition* 1989;41(2):50–61.

Costello J. 'Milk and sugar – the first drugs.' *Townsend Letter For Doctors* December 1991, p.1050.

Colbin, A. *Food and Healing* (Ballantine Books) pp.148–160.

Jukka Karjalainen et al. 'A Bovine Albumin Peptide as a Possible Trigger of Insulin-Dependent Diabetes Mellitus.' 1992;327:302–307.

Sheikh M.S. et al. 'Gastrointestinal absorption of calcium from milk and calcium salts.' *J. Nutrition* 1972;317:532–536.

Abraham G. 'The Calcium Controversy.' *J. Appl. Nutrition.* 1982;34:69–73.

5th International Colloquium on Monounsaturated Fatty Acids. 17 and 18 February 1992.

Holborow P. 'Melanoma patients consume more polyunsaturated fat that people without melanoma.' *New Zealand Medical Journal* 27 November 1991 p.502.

Halliwell B. *Free Radicals and Food Additives.* (Taylor & Francis) 1991.

Willett W.C., Stampfer M.J., Manson J.E., Colditz G.A., Speizer F.E., Rosner B.A., Sampson L.A., Hennekens C.H. 'Intake of *trans* fatty acids and risk of coronary heart disease among women.' *The Lancet* 1993;341:581–585.

Recommended Reading

If you choose to read more about food combining, one thing you will discover is that almost every practitioner and every writer differs slightly in their view of how it should be done. The approach will depend to a great extent on their own experience and on which tutor they followed. Some are certainly far easier than others to understand but this doesn't mean that there is a right or wrong way. In all cases, however, you'll find that the 'Don't mix proteins with starches' rule is absolute. For the rest, it's really a question of finding which variations suit you best.

My own perspective has evolved from studying the works of as many acknowledged experts as possible and also from my experience in practice, i.e. finding out what helps my own patients the most.

Avoid any confusion by, first of all, sticking absolutely to the rule that proteins should never be mixed with starches and, as far as possible, maintaining a balanced intake by choosing one protein-based meal, one starch-based meal and one alkaline-forming meal each day. The most important thing to remember is that you are completely individual and different to everyone else. What suits you may not suit another and vice versa. It's worth repeating that the rules of healthy eating are not written in tablets of stone nor should they be followed with religious fervour or fanaticism. After all, what we are told is *not* good for us one day suddenly becomes good for us the next, so it isn't surprising that you, the consumer of all these 180° turns, get confused. I always believe it best to tailor dietary management and nutritional therapy of any kind to individual needs, with the enjoyment factor kept uppermost in the mind at all times! Follow the food combining basics as often and as well as you can, but don't become *obsessed* with getting it right. Relish in your new-found knowledge and new-found health.

Recommended Books

The Food Combining Diet by Kathryn Marsden (Thorsons 1993)

Author's Note: From the feedback received, it seems that *The Food Combining Diet* fulfilled its aim of clearing up much of the myth and confusion which previously surrounded food combining. It has also helped thousands of people to lose weight successfully without dieting. Contains plenty of general health and diet information too.

Food and Healing by Annemarie Colbin (Ballantine Books, New York 1986)

Author's Note: In my view, one of the best books on general nutrition. Hard to find in the U.K. but well worth hunting for.

Fit For Life by Harvey and Marilyn Diamond (Bantam Books 1987)

Author's Note: A perennial bestseller. Essentially American in style and, for some, perhaps a little extreme in places but nevertheless full of sound advice, humour and fun. Lots of first-rate food combining recipes, too.

A New Way of Eating by Marilyn Diamond (Bantam Books 1987)

Author's Note: A *Fit For Life* follow-up and just as good.

Food Combining for Health by Doris Grant and Jean Joice (Thorsons 1984)

Author's Note: The first book on the Hay System to be published for the popular market in the UK. Doris Grant is a dedicated follower of the original Hay System, which differs from my own approach in that it does not adopt the separate fruit rule.

Food Combining for Vegetarians by Jackie Le Tissier (Thorsons 1992)

Author's Note: The title says it all.

10 Day Clean-Up Plan by Leslie Kenton (Century 1986)

Author's Note: A great cleansing, revitalizing routine.

Bodyfit by Josh Salzmann (Thorsons 1992)

Author's Note: This is an excellent, easy-to-follow book on sensible exercise that does not promise or expect miracles.

Stress Busters by Robert Holden (Thorsons 1992)

Author's Note: A strategy for survival in an increasingly stressful world. Full of common-sense, fun and laughter. Highly recommended.

Candida Albicans: Yeast and Your Health by Gill Jacobs (Optima 1990).

Resources

~

BIOCARE

Superior quality vitamin and mineral supplements including GLA, probiotics, liquid chromium, B complex, multi-vitamins, antioxidants and vitamin C. Also fructolite (fructose powder), a natural sugar substitute ideal for recovering hypolglycaemics. Fast and reliable mail order service available. Contact: Biocare Ltd. 54 Northfield Road, King's Norton, Birmingham B30 1JH, England. Telephone: 021 433 3727.

BLACKMORES

Quality herbals, vitamins and minerals and antioxidants. From health food stores. In case of difficulty, contact one of the following addresses:

UK: Blackmores Ltd., Unit 7 Poyle Tech Centre, Willow Road, Poyle, Colnbrook, Bucks SL3 0PD, England. Telephone: 0753 683815.

Australia: Blackmores Ltd., 23 Roseberry Street, Balgowlah 2093, New South Wales, Australia. Telephone: (02) 949 1954.

New Zealand: Blackmores Laboratories Ltd., 2 Parkhead Place, Albany, Auckland, New Zealand. Telephone: (010) 64 9 4158585.

EVENING PRIMROSE OIL

For further information call the Evening Primrose Office on 071 498 8256.

NELSON & RUSSELL

Aromatherapy oils. From most good chemists and health food stores. For additional stockist information contact: Nelson & Russell, 5 Endeavour Way, Wimbledon, London SW19 9UH. Telephone: 081 946 8527.

TISSERAND

Aromatherapy products and essential oil diffusers. For stockist information contact: Aromatherapy Products Ltd., The Knoll Business Centre, Old Shorcham Road, Hove, East Sussex BN3 7GS, England. Telephone: 0273 412139.

WAYMASTER

Water filter jugs and replacement filter cartridges: Waymaster Ltd., Meadow Road, Reading, Berkshire RG1 8LB, England. Telephone: 0734 599444. Contact them for details of local stockists.

BRAUN

Juicing machines and food processing equipment. For stockists contact: Braun UK Ltd., Dolphin Estate, Windmill Road, Sunbury-on- Thames, Middlesex TW16 7EJ, England. Telephone: 0932 785611.

NON-HYDROGENATED SPREADS

Non-hydrogenated spreads such as Vitaquell are available from most health food stores. Further details from the UK distributors: Brewhurst Health Food Supplies, Abbot Close, Oyster Lane, Byfleet, Surrey KT14 7JP, England. Telephone: 0932 354211.

ORGANIC FOOD SUPPLIES

The Soil Association, 86 Colston Street, Bristol, Avon BS1 5BB, England. Telephone: 0272 290661. Regional Guides available giving information relating to stockists, opening times, types of produce sold, delivery and mail order services county by county.

AMWAY

Suppliers of rebounders and deodorizing cleaning fluid. For details of nearest distributor, write to: Amway Information Centre, Snowdon Drive, Winterhill, Milton Keynes, Bucks. MK6 1AR, England. Telephone: 0908 691588. Amway products are available worldwide.

TEA AND COFFEE

Top-quality tea and coffee, all kinds including herbal and green teas, jasmine etc. by mail order from: Kendricks Coffee Co. Ltd., Tea and Coffee Specialists, Ocean Parade, South Ferring, Worthing, West Sussex BN12 5QQ. Telephone: 0903 503244 for mail order catalogue and price list.

COLD-PRESSED HONEYS

If you can't find cold-pressed honey in your health food store, contact: West Country Honey Farms, Braeside, Haydon Drove, West Horrington, Wells, Somerset BA5 3EH. Telephone: 04353 3638.

APPLE CIDER VINEGAR

Good-quality apple cider vinegar is available from good health food stores and delicatessens, but in case of difficulty contact: Martlet, Horham Manor, Horham, Heathfield, East Sussex TN21 0JA. Telephone: 04353 3638.

QUALITY BEE PRODUCTS

Good-quality bee products including pollen, honey and bee propolis should also be available from health food stores, but for stockist information contact: New Zealand Natural Food Co. Limited, 9 Holt Close, Highgate Wood, London N10 3HW. Telephone: 081 444 5660.

Index